COME
DANCE
WITH ME

Devotions for Deeper
Intimacy with God

GRETCHEN SCHWARTZMAN

Scripture quotations taken from the (NASB®) New American Standard Bible®, Copyright © 1960, 1971, 1977, 1995, 2020 by The Lockman Foundation. Used by permission. All rights reserved. lockman.org

First Printing Edition, 2024

ISBN:
979-8-9904847-0-2 (eBook)
979-8-9904847-1-9 (paperback)
979-8-9904847-2-6 (hardcover)

Heart Songs
PUBLISHING HOUSE
...BY THE WORD OF THEIR TESTIMONIES

PRAISE FOR *COME DANCE WITH ME*

"Devotionals that truly assist me as I pursue intimacy with Jesus are the ones that present both God's word in Scripture and also a personal invitation to encounter Him in prayer. Gretchen's work does this with clarity and balance. Her writing reflects a deep understanding and reverence for the written Word of God but also an intimate look into the interior whispers of God's Spirit as she meditates upon His presence. This book is a trustworthy guide to an affectionate and attentive prayer time."

—Matt Lozano, Associate Director, Heart of the Father Ministries and author

* * * * *

"Gretchen Schwartzman's 'Come Dance With Me' reads like a meditation and a consistent reminder to center our daily walk with Christ by setting our hearts and minds 'on things above, where Christ is, seated at the right hand of God'. For our times, this book is an engaging read like Andrew Murray's Abide in Christ was for his.

—Seema Freer, Ph.D., Leadership team and wife of lead pastor, Living Word Community

* * * * *

"I highly recommend Gretchen Schwartzman's book 'Come Dance with Me.' Besides being very well written, it leads us not only into God's presence but into a deeper intimacy with God. A must read.

—Lorenzo Bendlin, former missionary to Italy with WEC International

"This is a great book for spending a few minutes each day learning about your relationship with Jesus! Each brief devotion has a verse listed with it. From love, to spending time, to listening, to being obedient - all things that you can use to become more intimate with God. A great purchase to help develop your spiritual life!"

—Amy Shaw, Regional Area Coordinator,
Operation Christmas Child, a project of Samaritan's Purse

* * * * *

"This is truly a great read. Even though I'm halfway through, I cannot wait to read it once again! Truly excited to be able to recommend this devotional to others! I truly recommend this to be part of everyone's godly spiritual library as part of a daily devotional regimen.

—William Cepeda, Area Coordinator,
Operation Christmas Child, a project of Samaritan's Purse

* * * * *

"I was pleasantly surprised how Gretchen's devotional touched my spirit. I have been reading one or two pages a day to meditate on its deeper meaning. In particular, the devotion 'Quietness, Trust, Rest, and Joy' inspired joy that I later shared with a disabled child in my class. Thank you, Gretchen!"

—Joan H., veteran cross cultural worker

* * * * *

"I'm going through these pages in the mornings. In contemplation with Scripture, it has given me an unexpected slowing down as I take time to listen. I am really enjoying this and in hearing God, I find it leads to feeling closer. I recommend this book to those who wish to draw nearer!"

—Katherine, missionary to Eastern Europe

TABLE OF CONTENTS

PREFACE

One of the things that the Lord has been teaching me in recent years is to hear His voice. He clearly spoke to me at the beginning of Lenten season a few years ago and said that during the forty days of Lent He wanted me to spend at least five minutes each day (sometimes it would be much longer) just being still and quiet and listening to Him. This was not to be a time of reading His Word, although that is certainly vitally important. It was not a time of talking to Him in prayer and intercession, although that is also very necessary. It was to be a time of stillness, of waiting upon Him and learning to hear His voice. As I began to hear the Lord speak to me, I felt I needed to write down the words He gave me—mainly so I could remember them myself. (My memory is not as good as it used to be). I certainly had no initial intention of publishing these words for others to read. But as I have continued this discipline of being quiet before God and listening to Him, He has put it on my heart to share some of these words He has given me, first with my church and now in the printing of this book.

One of the frequent themes of these writings is intimacy with God. He has created us for intimacy with Himself. Adam and Eve enjoyed true intimacy with God in the garden before the fall. Ever since then, humanity has been seeking that intimacy which was lost. In this present age, Jesus has opened the door for that intimacy to be restored, and the Holy Spirit teaches us and leads us into that intimate relationship with God that our hearts long for. It is my sincere prayer that as you read these devotions, God will use them in some small way to draw you into a deeper more profound intimacy with Him—because in the end that is all that really matters.

ON LISTENING TO GOD

While working on the draft for this book, a dear sister in the Lord who had volunteered to read the draft and give me feedback made the suggestion that I write a section about how to listen to God since many people want to hear from God but struggle with how to do that. My first response was to be incredibly intimidated. I certainly do not consider myself to be an expert on hearing from God. I am still very much on the journey (and I'm sure I always will be for the rest of this lifetime). I thought to myself, "Who am I to write something on how to listen to God?" Then God spoke to me, "It is no different than writing all the devotions in this book. Look to Me, depend on Me, rely on Me. I will give you the words and the ideas to write." So by the grace of God and by the power of His Spirit, I give you a few pointers to help and encourage you in your journey of learning to hear God's voice.

Be intentional about setting aside regular time to practice listening to God even if it's just five minutes per day. Give God the best of your time when you are most awake and alert, not the leftovers of your time when you are exhausted and ready to fall asleep. If that means getting up a few minutes earlier in the morning, determine to do that. Your Father, the King of the Universe, wants to meet with you. Certainly that is worth making the effort to get up a little earlier. Try to find a place where you can have silence and the least amount of distractions possible. Do whatever you need to do to guard that time - hold it as sacred.

Be expectant. Expect God to speak to you. Jesus says in John 10:27 "My sheep hear My voice, and I know them, and they follow Me." Clearly His plan is that He would speak to us and that we would hear His voice and follow. Meditate on this verse. Cultivate a belief that Jesus will speak to you. If you have made Him Lord of your life, then you are one of His sheep. He will surely speak to you, and it is His will and desire that you listen and learn to hear His voice. Some books that have helped and encouraged me to have greater faith that God really will speak to me are: He Speaks in the Silence by Diane Comer, Come Away My Beloved by Frances J Roberts, and Jesus Calling by Sarah Young.

Be in the scriptures. One of the main ways that God speaks to us is through His Word, so having a plan to regularly read, memorize, and meditate on scripture is invaluable. God may speak to you through His Word as you prayerfully read it, or He may bring to mind a verse that you have previously memorized or have recently read and speak it to your heart as you are sitting in silence listening to Him. I have memorized quite a bit of scripture in my lifetime, and I find that many times God will bring these scriptures to my mind and apply them to a current situation in my life as I sit in silence before Him.

Be prayerful. Ask Jesus to teach you as one of His sheep to hear, to know, and to recognize His voice and to live listening to Him as a way of life. Pray this every day. God promises in His Word that if we ask anything according to His will, He hears us (1 John 5:14). Certainly, this is according to His will. Also, when I come before the Lord just to be still and silent and listen to Him, I pray the prayer of Samuel in 1 Samuel 3:9-10: "Speak, Lord, for Your servant is listening." This helps to open up my heart and mind to receive whatever God wants to speak to me and to focus on Him.

Be willing to obey and to act on what He speaks to you. God often speaks to us words of encouragement and comfort reminding us of His love and mercy and His many promises. But He also speaks words that require us to act - words about how to walk with Him and how to love and live with those around us. If we truly desire to hear God's voice, we must have hearts, minds, and wills disposed to humbly by the power of His Spirit set to obey what He speaks to us.

Write it down. I began writing down many of the things that God was speaking to me in my times of waiting for Him simply so that I could remember them. I found that by noon my over-fifty brain could forget what God had spoken to me in my quiet time early that morning. As you begin to hear Him speaking to you, you will want to remember and hang on to what He has said so that you can walk in it and apply it to your life. Often times I find that as I begin to write down what I have heard Him speak, more will come. It is also a great encouragement and reminder as well as a challenge to me to read back over the words He has spoken to me previously. It helps me to see how well I am tracking with what He is wanting to work into my life.

Be patient. This is not something you can learn in a day or a month or even a year. It is the journey of a lifetime, but it is the most rewarding journey you will ever embark on. Be patient with yourself. Not everyone learns at the same rate and not everyone hears God in exactly the same way. God has created each one of us to be a unique individual, and His relationship with each of us is unique. I know one dear brother in the Lord who often hears God speak to him during corporate worship. Another sister sometimes hears God speak to her through dreams. Others "hear" God speak to them through visions - God gives them a picture in their mind of something He wants them to know or understand. My best times of hearing from God have been when I am alone with Him in silence - He speaks into my heart and mind the words that He has for me. God knows each of us intimately and individually. He knows the words we need to hear and He knows how to best communicate them to us. Let us trust Him to teach us, lead us, and guide us on this path. If we are persistent to seek Him in this area, we will grow. Finally, you must first have a personal relationship with God through His Son Jesus. You must acknowledge that Jesus died for your sins, believe that He rose from the dead, and ask Him to come into your heart and be Lord of your life. This is the foundation for this journey.

Do Not Hold Back

Do not be afraid, do not think it is presumptuous to desire intimacy with Me, to desire to hear Me speak to you. This is what I died for. This is why—the whole purpose for which I sent My Son to bear your sins and suffer and die on the cross—to restore your relationship, your fellowship, your intimacy with Me—so that you can come right into the Holy of Holies, right before the throne of grace with confidence—so that you can expect to hear My voice and have intimate fellowship with Me. I have created you to have intimate fellowship with Me, and I long for that far more than you do. I have done this to restore that intimacy that I had with Adam when I walked and talked with him in the garden. Do not be afraid to approach Me, to draw near to Me, to listen to Me, to expect Me to speak to you. Do not hold back.

And behold, the veil of the temple was torn in two from top to bottom; and the earth shook and the rocks were split.

~Matthew 27:51

[19] Therefore, brethren, since we have confidence to enter the holy place by the blood of Jesus, [20] by a new and living way which He inaugurated for us through the veil, that is, His flesh, [21] and since we have a great priest over the house of God, [22] let us draw near with a sincere heart in full assurance of faith, having our hearts sprinkled clean from an evil conscience and our bodies washed with pure water.

~Hebrews 10:19-22

DEEPER WATERS

You are My child, and you are precious in My sight. Continue to press into Me – to go into deeper waters. Let your dance and worship be the overflow expression of a heart and life that is completely devoted to Me. I love you. Surrender yourself, abandon yourself to Me, and I will continue to use you in ways beyond what you are even aware of like an ever-widening circular ripple that spreads out from a single stone being thrown into water. Trust Me. Believe that I will do it. I am able to do, exceeding abundantly beyond all that you ask and think.

Now to Him who is able to do far more abundantly beyond all that we ask or think, according to the power that works within us

~Ephesians 3:20

DANCE WITH JESUS

When you dance at church, be sure you are really dancing with Me. I am using you to give people a glimpse of what it will look like to dance with Me in heaven. You will be dancing with Me for all eternity! Let your joy shine forth! Rejoice and dance with Jesus!

So the ransomed of the Lord will return
And come with joyful shouting to Zion,
And everlasting joy will be on their heads.
They will obtain gladness and joy,
And sorrow and sighing will flee away.

~Isaiah 51:11

² Let Israel be glad in his Maker;
Let the sons of Zion rejoice in their King.
³ Let them praise His name with dancing;
Let them sing praises to Him with timbrel and lyre.

~Psalm 149:2-3

QUIETNESS, TRUST, REST, AND JOY

My child, this is **My** plan for your life: quietness, trust, repentance, rest, unspeakable deep abiding joy. As you walk with Me, abide in Me, go deeper with Me, press on to know Me more intimately, this will be the natural outcome and outflow of your life. This is a picture of what your life should look like – keep it ever before you and believe Me to work it in you.

The steadfast of mind You will keep in perfect peace,
Because he trusts in You.
Trust in the Lord forever
For in God the Lord we have an everlasting Rock.

~Isaiah 26:3-4

In repentance and rest you will be saved,
In quietness and trust is your strength.

~Isaiah 30:15

And the ransomed of the Lord will return
And come with joyful shouting to Zion,
With everlasting joy upon their heads.
They will find gladness and joy
And sorrow and sighing will flee away.

~Isaiah 35:10

You will make known to me the path of life;
In Your presence is fullness of joy;
In Your right hand there are pleasures forever.

~Psalms 16:11

LISTEN TO ME

I want to speak to you. I desire to speak to you every day if you will but listen. My speaking to you should not be the exception reserved for special occasions. It should be the norm – the pattern of your daily life.

You absolutely are one of My sheep and you absolutely are able to hear and know and recognize My voice. And I absolutely am speaking to you, but you must learn to listen and hear My voice by practicing every day. Be **intentional** about listening to Me.

*³ To him the doorkeeper opens, and the sheep hear his voice,
and he calls his own sheep by name and leads them out.
⁴ When he puts forth all his own, he goes ahead of them,
and the sheep follow him because they know his voice.*

²⁷ My sheep hear My voice, and I know them, and they follow Me;

~John 10:3-4, 27

DANCE BY MY SPIRIT

You *can* dance with a right heart, a pure heart before Me whether dancing up front during worship time in the church service or in your personal devotional time. Just do it by My Spirit. Let My Spirit have free reign in you. Let My Spirit be the One dancing in and through you, and your heart will be right before Me and your worship will be a pleasing offering and sacrifice unto Me.

And do not neglect to worship Me with dance in your own personal devotional times with Me. If you want to be a true worshipper and a true worship dancer, you must come before Me with dance in your own quiet times.

23 But an hour is coming, and now is, when the true worshipers will worship the Father in spirit and truth; for such people the Father seeks to be His worshipers. 24 God is spirit, and those who worship Him must worship in spirit and truth."

~John 4:23-24

*6 Then he said to me,
"This is the word of the Lord to Zerubbabel saying,
'Not by might nor by power,
but by My Spirit,' says the Lord of hosts.*

~Zechariah 4:6

Renewing Love

My child, bask in My presence and drink in deeply of My love and be refreshed and renewed. My love truly is like a waterfall to renew and refresh and revive you soul.

I have loved you with an everlasting love,
Therefore I have drawn you with lovingkindness.

~Jeremiah 31:3

The Lord's lovingkindnesses indeed never cease,
For His compassions never fail.
They are new every morning.
Great is Your faithfulness.

~Lamentations 3:22-23

And hope does not disappoint, because the love of God
has been poured out within our hearts through the
Holy Spirit who was given to us.

~Romans 5:5

My Grace is Enough

My grace truly is enough. Do you really believe that? My grace is enough for you when you are frustrated at your spouse or your co-worker. My grace is enough for you when you are irritated with your mother or father, brother or sister, your child, or your neighbor. My grace is deeper and wider than the sea. My grace is inexhaustible – it will never run out. By My grace you can stand through whatever you have to deal with in your life. My grace is enough.

[9] And He has said to me, "My grace is sufficient for you, for power is perfected in weakness." Most gladly, therefore, I will rather boast about my weaknesses, so that the power of Christ may dwell in me. [10] Therefore I am well content with weaknesses, with insults, with distresses, with persecutions, with difficulties, for Christ's sake; for when I am weak, then I am strong.

~2 Corinthians 12:9-10

JUST BE

It gives Me great, great joy and so much pleasure when you come just to spend time with Me and to be in My presence. This is what you were made for, what you were created for. Come into My presence and just be, just enjoy Me. Even right now at this very moment, come into My presence and just be, just enjoy Me.

[8] My soul clings to You;
Your right hand upholds me.

~Psalm 63:8

[1] You will make known to me the path of life;
In Your presence is fullness of joy;
In Your right hand there are pleasures forever.

~Psalm 16:11

Constant Communion

Just as I, God the Father, Son, and Holy Spirit, dwell in constant unbroken loving fellowship as the Holy Trinity, so have I created you in My image. I have made you and created you to dwell in unbroken loving fellowship with Me. It is My plan, My will, My desire for you to live in constant intimate communion with Me – for us to enjoy continual intimate fellowship with one another.

[26] Then God said, "Let Us make man in Our image, according to Our likeness; and let them rule over the fish of the sea and over the birds of the sky and over the cattle and over all the earth, and over every creeping thing that creeps on the earth." [27] God created man in His own image, in the image of God He created him; male and female He created them.

~Gen 1:26-27

*[9] Just as the Father has loved Me,
I have also loved you; abide in My love.*

~John 15:9

LIVE IN THE PRESENT

My daughter, my son, do not live in the past. You cannot change it. You can learn from the past, but you cannot redo it; it is done. Do not spend your time mulling over it or dwelling on it.

Do not live in the future for the future holds no guarantees. You do not know what the future will bring.

Live in the present; live for today. And live every day, every moment, fully for Me and with Me. I give you today. It is My gift to you. Live it to the fullest; live it with Me. Enjoy it and be thankful.

[18] "Do not call to mind the former things,
Or ponder things of the past.
[19] "Behold, I will do something new,
Now it will spring forth;
Will you not be aware of it?
I will even make a roadway in the wilderness,
Rivers in the desert.

~Isaiah 43:18-19

[34] "So do not worry about tomorrow; for tomorrow will
care for itself. Each day has enough trouble of its own.

~Matthew 6:34

COME AWAY AND BE WITH ME

Do not forget how quickly and how easily you can be knocked off course and lose sight of Me. You need to spend time with Me to refocus every day. Do not underestimate the power of the world to cloud your vision. I am your Source. The Holy Spirit is your lifeline that connects you to Me. You need to just be with Me and to be freshly filled with My Spirit every day. If you neglect this, it will be to the detriment of your faith. I am here waiting to spend time with you every day. Come away. Be with Me. Drink in deeply of Me. Let Me renew your vision and your perspective.

¹⁸ And do not get drunk with wine,
for that is dissipation, but be filled with the Spirit,

~Ephesians 5:18

³⁷ Now on the last day, the great day of the feast, Jesus stood and cried out, saying, "If anyone is thirsty, let him come to Me and drink. ³⁸ He who believes in Me, as the Scripture said, 'From his innermost being will flow rivers of living water.'"

~John 7:37-38

Total Surrender

Father, thank You for creating me, for giving me life and breath, for calling me to Yourself, for adopting me into Your family, for setting me apart, for making me Yours. Father, I am Yours. I belong to You wholly, completely, unreservedly. You are the only One who has the right to all of me. You bought me. You own me. I am Yours – period.

I have loved you with an everlasting love,
Therefore I have drawn you with lovingkindness.

~Jeremiah 31:3

I have called you by name. You are Mine!

~Isaiah 43:1

Persevere in Prayer

When you pray, I am listening, and I am already working. Though you may not see the answer yet, and you may not see it for quite some time, nevertheless I am already working to bring it to pass. Do not lose heart. Do not give up. Keep entrusting it to Me.

²² And all things you ask in prayer, believing, you will receive."

~Matthew 21:22

Hold Nothing Back

Do not be afraid to give everything to Me unreservedly, to hold nothing back, to obey Me in everything. Trust Me. I am your Father. I love you. I gave everything for you. I gave My Son for you. You can trust Me. I love you more than you can imagine. All My intentions toward you are good. All My plans for your life are good. You can trust in Me with your whole heart, which will enable you to also obey Me in everything. My son, My daughter, I love you.

¹¹ For I know the plans that I have for you,'
declares the LORD, 'plans for welfare and not
for calamity to give you a future and a hope.

~Jeremiah 29:11

²⁸ And we know that God causes all things to work
together for good to those who love God,
to those who are called according to His purpose.

~Romans 8:28

Only by My Spirit

This is the answer to the temptations both of pride and of fear related to self-reliance, independence, self-dependence, and control. When you are tempted to be proud of all your various accomplishments in ministry, remember that it is **only** by My Spirit that you can do **any** of the things you are doing for My kingdom, and only as you **completely** rely on My Spirit will you be doing them rightly as I desire. When you are tempted to be afraid—anxious and worried—that you can't do it all, that you can't keep it all together, remember that by My Spirit dwelling in you, you absolutely can do all that I have called you to do. Zechariah 4:6 is your secret to being both confident and humble in all the ways I have called you to serve Me.

'Not by might, nor by power,
but by My Spirit,' says the Lord of hosts.

~Zechariah 4:6

Take Time with Me

Take time to wait upon Me, to be still before Me, to focus on Me, to listen to Me. It is your lifeblood. The busier you are, the more you need to take time to sit before Me and to be in My presence.

Make sure that everything you are doing is of Me. If it is, then I <u>will</u> give you the strength and time to do it. "Not by might, nor by power, but by My Spirit."

¹⁶ But Jesus Himself would often
slip away to the wilderness and pray.

¹² It was at this time that He went off to the mountain to pray,
and He spent the whole night in prayer to God.

~Luke 5:16, 6:12

DEPEND COMPLETELY ON ME

I have put you in every one of the positions and ministries that you are in right now. You are there because I have called you to be there; I have appointed you.

I will give you everything you need to carry out these responsibilities, only depend **completely** on Me: My grace, My wisdom, My strength. Take time to spend with Me, to wait upon Me, to hear My voice, to be led by My Spirit. Humble yourself completely before Me, and absolutely despair of all your own abilities and strength and creativity and wisdom except as they are inspired and submitted and brought under the control of My Spirit.

*'Not by might, nor by power,
but by My Spirit,' says the Lord of hosts.*

~Zechariah 4:6

And He has said to me, "My grace is sufficient for you, for power is perfected in weakness." Most gladly, therefore, I will rather boast about my weaknesses, so that the power of Christ may dwell in me. Therefore I am well content with weaknesses, with insults, with distresses, with persecutions, with difficulties for Christ's sake, for when I am weak then I am strong.

~2 Corinthians 12:9-10

Spend Time in My Presence

You pray every day for Me to teach you to listen and to hear My voice, but you are not taking and making the time to wait upon Me, to be still before Me. Do not think that I am just going to drop that on you instantly. It takes **time** to learn to hear My voice. You must be willing to spend time in My presence waiting upon Me. And that is the only way to have a heart that is truly and wholly devoted to Me as David did.

¹⁴ Wait for the Lord;
Be strong and let your heart take courage;
Yes, wait for the Lord.

~Psalm 27:14

COME SIT BEFORE ME

Be still and know that I am God. This is a command, not an option. This is the most important thing that you should be about every day: to wait upon Me, to be still before Me, to listen to Me, to come into My presence and sit before Me as David did. David was a man after My own heart with a heart wholly devoted to Me. The expression and outworking and source of that was the time he spent meditating upon Me, sitting before Me. You can't have one without the other. They must go hand in hand. Even when David was king of the entire nation of Israel with many responsibilities, he made time to "go in and sit before the Lord."

18 Then David the king went in and sat before the Lord,
and he said, "Who am I, O Lord God,
and what is my house,
that You have brought me this far?

~2 Samuel 7:18

A Heart Wholly Devoted

Lessons from the life of David:

David brought the ark of the Lord into Jerusalem, and he danced before the Lord with all his might while that was taking place. He also established continual worship before the ark of God in Jerusalem. When God promised David that He would establish David's kingdom forever, David went in and sat before the Lord with a thankful and grateful and humble heart. Before going into battle, David always inquired of the Lord whether they should go and if the Lord would give the enemy into their hands. Except for the incidents of Bathsheba and the census which he repented of; David always obeyed God in everything. He wrote the Psalms to express his love and devotion to God. His heart was wholly devoted to God.

We see in 1 Chronicles 18 that as a result, God firmly established David's kingdom. David won every battle. God gave him success wherever he went and blessed him on every side.

A word from the Lord: The more your life is entirely intertwined with Me, the more My blessings will be released in your life.

God testified concerning him: I have found David son of Jesse, a man after my own heart; he will do everything I want him to do.

~Acts 13:22 NIV

LIFT UP YOUR EYES

When you wait upon Me and listen to Me, do so expectantly. Lift up your eyes to Me, and expect Me to speak. Expect to hear from Me.

I will lift up my eyes to the mountains;
From where shall my help come?
² My help comes from the Lord,
Who made heaven and earth.

~Psalm 121:1-2

BE EXPECTANT

Do not put limits or boundaries on how I can speak to you. I am much bigger than you think. Be expectant. I speak in many different ways. Look for Me to speak to you in My Word, through the circumstances of your life, through other people, through My creation, through a song that you hear, and in other ways that you have not even imagined. Stay open and expect to hear Me in every way I would choose to speak to you throughout your day.

*19 The heavens are telling of the glory of God;
And their expanse is declaring the work of His hands.*

~Psalm 19:1

*105 Your word is a lamp to my feet
And a light to my path.*

~Psalm 119:105

*Without consultation, plans are frustrated,
But with many counselors they succeed.*

~Proverbs 15:22 NIV

SET YOUR HEART

In order to truly please Me and walk uprightly, you must <u>set</u> <u>your</u> <u>heart</u> to seek Me. It's all about your heart. Where is your heart?

Because Jehoshaphat sought Me with his whole heart and sought to fully obey Me in all that he did, I blessed the entire nation of Judah. By his devotion and obedience, the lives of everyone in the nation were touched and blessed.

To the degree that you seek Me with your whole heart and seek to obey Me in all that I have called you to do, I will use you to touch and to be a blessing in the lives of many around you.

[14] He did evil because he did not set his heart to seek the LORD.

~2 Chronicles 12:14

Jehoshaphat Succeeds Asa

Jehoshaphat his son then became king in his place, and made his position over Israel firm. [2] He placed troops in all the fortified cities of Judah, and set garrisons in the land of Judah and in the cities of Ephraim which Asa his father had captured.

His Good Reign

³ The Lord was with Jehoshaphat because he followed the example of his father David's earlier days and did not seek the Baals, ⁴ but sought the God of his father, followed His commandments, and did not act as Israel did. ⁵ So the Lord established the kingdom in his control, and all Judah brought tribute to Jehoshaphat, and he had great riches and honor. ⁶ He took great pride in the ways of the Lord and again removed the high places and the Asherim from Judah.

⁷ Then in the third year of his reign he sent his officials, Ben-hail, Obadiah, Zechariah, Nethanel and Micaiah, to teach in the cities of Judah; ⁸ and with them the Levites, Shemaiah, Nethaniah, Zebadiah, Asahel, Shemiramoth, Jehonathan, Adonijah, Tobijah and Tobadonijah, the Levites; and with them Elishama and Jehoram, the priests. ⁹ They taught in Judah, having the book of the law of the Lord with them; and they went throughout all the cities of Judah and taught among the people.

¹⁰ Now the dread of the Lord was on all the kingdoms of the lands which were around Judah, so that they did not make war against Jehoshaphat. ¹¹ Some of the Philistines brought gifts and silver as tribute to Jehoshaphat; the Arabians also brought him flocks, 7,700 rams and 7,700 male goats. ¹² So Jehoshaphat grew greater and greater, and he built fortresses and store cities in Judah. ¹³ He had large supplies in the cities of Judah, and warriors, valiant men, in Jerusalem. ¹⁴ This was their muster according to their fathers' households: of Judah, commanders of thousands, Adnah was the commander, and with him 300,000 valiant warriors; ¹⁵ and next to him was Johanan the commander, and with him 280,000; ¹⁶ and next to him Amasiah the son of Zichri, who volunteered for the Lord, and with him 200,000 valiant warriors; ¹⁷ and of Benjamin, Eliada a valiant warrior, and with him 200,000 armed with bow and shield; ¹⁸ and next to him Jehozabad, and with him 180,000 equipped for war. ¹⁹ These are they who served the king, apart from those whom the king put in the fortified cities through all Judah.

~2 Chronicles 17

Leave It in My Hands

I hold the hearts of kings in My hands—also the hearts of presidents, supreme court justices, governors, and all world leaders. How much more am I in control of every detail of your life. So, trust Me. **Really** trust Me. Do not be anxious or worried. Do what you need to do, but leave it in My hands, and trust in Me for every detail of your life. I am in control of the small things and the big things, the details of your personal life and the things that are going on in the whole world. I am in control of all. So, you can entrust everything to Me.

The king's heart is like channels of water in the hand of the Lord;
He turns it wherever He wishes.

~Proverbs 21:1

29 Are not two sparrows sold for a cent? And yet not one of them
will fall to the ground apart from your Father.
30 But the very hairs of your head are all numbered.
31 So do not fear; you are more valuable than many sparrows.

~Matthew 10:29-31

LISTEN TO ME DAILY

Don't be anxious about hearing Me. Trust in Me. I am <u>pleased</u> when you come before Me to wait upon Me, to listen to Me. That causes Me no end of joy, and I will surely bless you and speak to you as you show yourself faithful to come before Me to listen to Me every day.

³ Glory in His holy name;
Let the heart of those who seek the LORD be glad.
⁴ Seek the LORD and His strength;
Seek His face continually.

~Psalm 105:3-4

Obedience and Hearing

Mary clearly heard Me speak to her and her response was, "Behold the handmaid of the Lord. Be it unto me according to Thy word."

She already had a heart disposed to obey, and she was able to hear Me clearly. The more you practice walking in obedience to Me and make it part of your daily everyday life, the more you will be able to hear and discern My voice.

38 And Mary said, "Behold, the bondslave of the Lord;
may it be done to me according to your word."
And the angel departed from her.

~Luke 1:38

TRUST IN ME

Trust in Me for what concerns you right now.

Do not fear, for I am with you;
Do not anxiously look about you,
for I am your God.
I will strengthen you,
surely I will help you,
Surely I will uphold you with My righteous right hand.

~Isaiah 41:10

Trust the Lord with all your heart
And do not lean on your own understanding.
In all your ways acknowledge Him,
And He will make your paths straight.

~Proverbs 3:5-6

The Outpouring of My Spirit

Do not fear, do not hesitate or hold back, in putting all your hope and trust in Me. You will never be disappointed. I already have and will continuously every day **pour out My love** into your heart by My Spirit whom I have given to you. By My Spirit within you, you can know the fullness of My love for you, and you really do have the fullness of My love in your heart to be able to love Me, your brothers and sisters, your neighbors, your co-workers.

"Not by might, nor by power, but by My Spirit." The secret is My Spirit—complete, utter, absolute surrender and abandonment to Me—to be filled with My Spirit, walk by My Spirit, live every moment in My Spirit.

Yes, Lord. Fill me up, Lord. Fill me up. Fill me up until I overflow. Fill me up up up up. Fill me up to the brim. Fill me up all the way with your Holy Spirit—totally and completely and entirely.

⁵ and hope does not disappoint, because the love of God has been poured out within our hearts through the Holy Spirit who was given to us.

~Romans 5:5

⁶ Then he said to me, "This is the word of the Lord to Zerubbabel saying, 'Not by might nor by power, but by My Spirit,' says the Lord of hosts.

~Zechariah 4:6

Enjoy My Presence

Spending time in My presence, waiting upon Me, listening to Me should never be a drudge or a duty. It should never be a source of anxiety or feeling like you "have to" hear something. It is a **relationship**. Just enjoy being with Me. Enjoy being in My presence whether you hear Me speak or not. It brings joy to My heart just that you have come to sit before Me, to be in My presence. I enjoy being with you.

Be still, and know that I am God.

~Psalms 46:10 (NIV)

In Your presence is fullness of joy.

~Psalms 16:11

Delight yourself in the Lord;
And He will give you the desires of your heart.

~Psalms 37:4

THE GIFT OF MY SPIRIT

See what a precious and priceless gift I have given you in the gift of My Spirit. Not only are you transferred instantly from the kingdom of darkness to the kingdom of Light by My Spirit, but you are also given the power and the grace to continually walk in the Light, to bask in the Light, to reflect the Light, to be filled with Light, to shine forth the Light.

[12] Then Jesus again spoke to them, saying,
"I am the Light of the world;
he who follows Me will not walk in the darkness,
but will have the Light of life.

~John 8:12

[14] "You are the light of the world. A city set on a hill cannot be hidden; [15] nor does anyone light a lamp and put it under a basket, but on the lampstand, and it gives light to all who are in the house. [16] Let your light shine before men in such a way that they may see your good works, and glorify your Father who is in heaven.

~Matthew 5:14-16

[16] But I say, walk by the Spirit,
and you will not carry out the desire of the flesh.

~Galatians 5:16

POINT PEOPLE TO ME

I am the only way to the Father, the only way to eternal life. People need to believe in Me, to know Me in order to have eternal life. You need to tell them, to let them know, to point them to Me. Everything about your life, all that you do and say, should point people to Me.

Expect Me to be working in your life, I always am.

Expect Me to be speaking into your heart, I always do.

Expect Me to be transforming your thoughts, I always am.

I am the way, and the truth, and the life;
no one comes to the Father but through Me.

~John 14:6

The Call to Go Deeper

Come. Sit on My lap. Lean your head against My breast. Enjoy being held by Me. Enjoy being in My presence.

Really learning to hear Me is all about really knowing Me—true intimacy with Me, being vulnerable to Me, opening your heart completely to Me. Deep calls to deep. Are you ready to go there?

⁷ Deep calls to deep at the sound of Your waterfalls;
All Your breakers and Your waves have rolled over me.
⁸ The Lord will command His lovingkindness in the daytime;
And His song will be with me in the night,
A prayer to the God of my life.

~Psalm 42:7-8

Then he brought me back to the door of the house; and behold, water was flowing from under the threshold of the house toward the east, for the house faced east. And the water was flowing down from under, from the right side of the house, from south of the altar. ² He brought me out by way of the north gate and led me around on the outside to the outer gate by way of the gate that faces east. And behold, water was trickling from the south side.

³ When the man went out toward the east with a line in his hand, he measured a thousand cubits, and he led me through the water, water reaching the ankles. ⁴ Again he measured a thousand and led me through the water, water reaching the knees. Again he measured a thousand and led me through the water, water reaching the loins. ⁵ Again he measured a thousand; and it was a river that I could not ford, for the water had risen, enough water to swim in, a river that could not be forded.

~Ezekiel 47:1-5

SMALL STEPS

I will not give you more than what you can do, more than what you can manage. I will give you small steps that you can take every day, only be faithful in the small things. Be faithful to carry out those things that I have placed on your heart and spoken into your life. Then you will reap the rewards of true intimacy with Me. As you listen, learn to hear My voice, **and** obey.

[21] His master said to him, 'Well done, good and faithful slave. You were faithful with a few things, I will put you in charge of many things; enter into the joy of your master.'

~Matthew 25:21

FIX YOUR ATTENTION ON ME

Keep your full attention focused on Me. You so easily and quickly get distracted by other things—even trying to figure out how to do good or be a blessing to others. Fix your whole heart, your whole mind, your whole will only on Me. **I** will show you how **I** want to use you to be a blessing to others.

[41] But the Lord answered and said to her, "Martha, Martha, you are worried and bothered about so many things;
[42] but only one thing is necessary, for Mary has chosen the good part, which shall not be taken away from her."

~Luke 10:41-42

Be On Guard

My child, do you see how easily and how quickly you can fall out of the habit of listening to Me? Do not think you can coast on your past experiences. Every day you must determine anew to listen to Me for whatever I have to speak to you for **that day**. Be alert! Be on guard! There is nothing Satan would rather do than pull you away from listening to Me and communing with Me. But I have called you and ordained you and created you for intimacy with Me, and I will give you the grace to pursue that and to walk in that. Nothing in life is sweeter than walking in intimate fellowship with Me.

[13] "Oh that My people would listen to Me,
That Israel would walk in My ways!

~Psalm 81:13

BE A CHANNEL FOR MY LOVE

True love really does transcend all, and I am the one true source of love. Let yourself become a channel for My love. Drink it in deeply. Immerse yourself in it. Wallow in it. You cannot have too much of My love. But also let Me love others through you. Look around. Who can you show My love to today? When you are showing My love and doing acts of love to bless others in the power of My Spirit, then you are really revealing Me to them. They will see Me in you.

19 We love, because He first loved us.

~1 John 4:19

22 Since you have in obedience to the truth purified your souls for a sincere love of the brethren, fervently love one another from the heart.

~1 Peter 1:22

31 The second is this, 'You shall love your neighbor as yourself.' There is no other commandment greater than these."

~Mark 12:31

PEACE IN MY PRESENCE

You can be more comfortable spending time with Me than with anyone else. I am your Father who made you. I know you inside and outside. I know all your thoughts and the deepest desires of your heart. I know everything about you. You can rest and relax in My presence. Be at peace. Just be.

O Lord, You have searched me and known me.
² You know when I sit down and when I rise up;
You understand my thought from afar.
³ You scrutinize my path and my lying down,
And are intimately acquainted with all my ways.
⁴ Even before there is a word on my tongue,
Behold, O Lord, You know it all.
⁵ You have enclosed me behind and before,
And laid Your hand upon me.
⁶ Such knowledge is too wonderful for me;
It is too high, I cannot attain to it.

¹⁵ My frame was not hidden from You,
When I was made in secret,
And skillfully wrought in the depths of the earth;
¹⁶ Your eyes have seen my unformed substance;
And in Your book were all written
The days that were ordained for me,
When as yet there was not one of them.

[17] How precious also are Your thoughts to me, O God!
How vast is the sum of them!
[18] If I should count them, they would outnumber the sand.
When I awake, I am still with You.

~Psalm 139:1-6, 15-18

GIVE ME EACH DAY

My child, **every day** you have a new opportunity to go deeper with Me, to walk more closely with Me, to abide more consistently in My presence, to live listening to Me and to hear My voice. Each day is a fresh start. Each day you have the chance to grow closer to Me, to know Me better. In your heart of hearts, you desire and long for true intimacy with Me. I know this because I have put that desire there. Know that a life of deepening intimacy with Me is built **one day at a time**. Give Me each day. Make that decision each day. Make walking with Me and talking with Me your first priority each day. And be expectant every single day that I will meet you, I will speak to you, and I will draw you closer to Me, to My heart. That is **My** greatest desire, and it is also the longing of **My** heart.

[7] For He is our God,
And we are the people of His pasture and the sheep of His hand.
Today, if you would hear His voice,
[8] Do not harden your hearts, as at Meribah,
As in the day of Massah in the wilderness

~Psalm 95:7-8

[8] Draw near to God and He will draw near to you. Cleanse your hands, you sinners; and purify your hearts, you double-minded.

~James 4:8a

Delight yourself in the Lord;
And He will give you the desires of your heart.

~Psalm 37:4

Be Real with Me

Relax! You don't have to perform for Me. You can be more real with Me than with anyone else. You can be totally yourself with Me. My love for you does not depend on anything you do or don't do. You can relax and be at ease in My presence. Your part is to come and put yourself before Me. I will do all the rest.

⁷ Rest in the Lord and wait patiently for Him;
Do not fret because of him who prospers in his way,
Because of the man who carries out wicked schemes.

~Psalm 37:7a

GIVE YOURSELF TO ME

Do not be afraid to know more about yourself, your personality, your underlying motivations, and your thought patterns. Give everything that you know and understand about yourself and all that you don't know to Me. I am big enough to handle all of it. I will change you. I will transform you. I will remake you as you entrust yourself to Me.

⁵ Commit your way to the Lord,
Trust also in Him, and He will do it.
⁶ He will bring forth your righteousness as the light
And your judgment as the noonday.

~Psalm 37:5-6

THE PATH TO THE HIGH PLACES

I know the path you need to follow to reach the high places. Everyone's path is a little bit different—no two are the same. I know the path you need to take because I have laid it out for you, and I see the whole path. Put your hand in Mine and walk with Me. As you trust in Me and walk hand in hand with Me, I will show you the way and keep you on the correct path.

[33] He makes my feet like hinds' feet,
And sets me upon my high places.

~Psalm 18:33

[19] The Lord God is my strength,
And He has made my feet like hinds' feet,
And makes me walk on my high places.

~Habakkuk 3:19

Take My Hand

See My hand. I am reaching out to you. Take My hand. Put your hand in Mine. I will never let you go. You can choose to take your hand out of Mine, but don't. Walk with Me hand in hand as Noah did, as Abraham did. I made a covenant with each of them. I have also made a covenant with you. It is a new covenant, a better covenant in the blood of My own Son Jesus so that you can walk with Me in a way even Noah and Abraham could not. So, take My hand. Walk side by side, hand in hand with Me every day. Let Me lead you and guide you to keep you on the right path. And when the path is difficult and rocky and steep, I will hold onto you and pull you up and even lift you over the really challenging places.

The LORD says, "I will guide you along the best pathway for your life. I will advise you and watch over you."

~Psalm 32:8 NLT

WALK WITH ME

I am reaching out My hand to you today. Put your hand in Mine today. Take My hand and don't let go, don't pull back. Walk with Me hand in hand all day today. You are at that point that you can do this because I have been preparing you. Make this walking with Me your first priority. Push through to the next level. I have been making your feet like hinds feet so that you can walk on the high places with Me.

Then Enoch walked with God three hundred years…
Enoch walked with God; and he was not, for God took him.

~Genesis 5:22-24

Noah was a righteous man, blameless in his time;
Noah walked with God.

~Genesis 6:9

CREATED FOR INTIMACY

Do you still doubt that you can really have intimacy with Me? Do you still not truly believe that I have created you for intimacy with Myself? Or do you think that type of intimacy is only for the "super Christians"—those select few who are super holy and devoted—and that you cannot attain to it? That is a lie that the enemy of your soul would like you to believe, but it is not true. Don't buy into it! I have indeed created **you** to have intimacy with Me, and I have opened the way for you to do that. I am calling you to that higher path, and I will not rest until you are walking with Me there. You are destined for this. Trust Me. Believe in Me. Put your hands in Mine and let Me bring you there.

⁵ Trust in the Lord with all your heart
And do not lean on your own understanding.
⁶ In all your ways acknowledge Him,
And He will make your paths straight.

~Proverbs 3:5-6

REFLECT ME

I am drawing you into a deeper intimacy with Me. And the closer and more intimate you are with Me, the more I will be reflected in your life. I have created you in My image. I have made you to reflect Me—to be just like My Son Jesus. This is your destiny. But I am the One who must set the pace and the tempo for this. I am the director and the conductor of your life. Trust in Me, wait upon Me, and put yourself entirely in My hands.

⁵ My soul, wait in silence for God only,
For my hope is from Him.

~Psalm 62:5

My soul clings to You;
Your right hand upholds me.

~Psalm 63:8

Walking the High Road

The reason the high road is glorious and full of light is because you are walking hand in hand with Me. Put your hand in Mine every day. Choose to take My hand and don't let go. Hold on for dear life for that is your lifeline. I will help you over the rocky places and carry you when the path is too steep. Only leave your hand in Mine. Do not snatch it away. You will see how I give you My perspective on every situation and enable you to live above your circumstances as you walk hand in hand with Me.

"If you'll hold on to me for dear life," says God,
"I'll get you out of any trouble. I'll give you the best
of care if you'll only get to know and trust me.

~Psalm 91:14 MSG

Give Me Your Time

Give Me the sacrifice of your time. Every moment of your life, every moment that you have life and breath, is a precious gift from Me. Offer it back to Me by spending time with Me, waiting upon Me, being still in My presence. Not only will you find great joy in My presence, but you will also bring great joy and blessing to Me, your Father. For I delight in you, and I take great delight in spending time with you.

Rest in the Lord and wait patiently for Him;
Do not fret because of him who prospers in his way,
Because of the man who carries out wicked schemes.

~Psalm 37:7a

Share Your Heart with Me

Listening is an important part of your relationship with Me. But it is also important to share with Me what is on your heart and mind. Yes it is true that I already know all of that, but it is important for you that you tell Me and share it with Me, so that you can know that I am listening and that I truly do care about every detail of your life. Tell Me all that you are thinking and feeling. I am the only One who can fully understand you, even to the very depths of your soul. And then listen for My response that we may have a true dialog and that you may enter into greater intimacy with Me.

I waited patiently for the Lord;
And He inclined to me and heard my cry.

~Psalm 40:1

CREATED TO WORSHIP

I have created you to worship Me. Worshiping Me, praising Me, adoring Me, enjoying Me, praying to Me, waiting upon Me, listening to Me, being in My presence is always the very best thing you can do. This is how you will spend all of eternity. It is as you worship Me that your heart, your mind, your soul, and your spirit are truly free.

I have given you the heart of a worshiper. This is where you are truly at home—when you are worshiping Me, adoring Me, being in My presence, basking in My love. Wherever you are physically, you are truly at home and your heart is at rest when you are worshiping and loving Me. I have created you this way.

23 But an hour is coming, and now is, when the true worshipers will worship the Father in spirit and truth; for such people the Father seeks to be His worshipers. 24 God is spirit, and those who worship Him must worship in spirit and truth."

~John 4:23-24

6 Come, let us worship and bow down,
Let us kneel before the Lord our Maker.
7 For He is our God,
And we are the people of His pasture and the sheep of His hand.
Today, if you would hear His voice,

~Psalm 95:6-7

14 And David was dancing before the Lord with all his might,
and David was wearing a linen ephod.
~2 Samuel 6:14

PLUG INTO MY POWER

I am your source of Power and strength for each day. Just as an electrical appliance can run and do what it was made to do only if it is plugged into a power source, so too you can live and walk through each day as I have created you to do only as you are "plugged in" to Me. Just as medical equipment has a backup battery that can run for a little while without being plugged in, so you may be able to coast and run for a while on your past spiritual experiences and encounters with Me. But you will not be able to sustain that—it will not last. You must plug into Me and be freshly empowered by My Spirit on a daily basis.

[4] Abide in Me, and I in you. As the branch cannot bear fruit of itself unless it abides in the vine, so neither can you unless you abide in Me. [5] I am the vine, you are the branches; he who abides in Me and I in him, he bears much fruit, for apart from Me you can do nothing.

~John 15:4-5

IRRESISTIBLE LOVE

I give you a heart to know Me, for I am the Lord. I have loved you with an everlasting love, therefore I draw you to Myself by My lovingkindness. It was Me who initially reached out to you and drew you unto Myself by My everlasting, immeasurable, infinite lovingkindness, and it is Me who continues to gently draw you closer, deeper, into greater intimacy with Me by My Spirit, by My irresistible love. I will keep you. I will not let go of you. You are Mine. I put the hunger and thirst in your heart for more of Me. Just open yourself up to Me, to My Spirit. Spend time with Me—that time is never a waste. You will find yourself in Me. The greatest longings of your heart will be satisfied in Me.

7 I will give them a heart to know Me, for I am the Lord;
and they will be My people, and I will be their God,
for they will return to Me with their whole heart.

~Jeremiah 24:7

3 The Lord appeared to him from afar, saying,
"I have loved you with an everlasting love;
Therefore I have drawn you with lovingkindness.

~Jeremiah 31:3

OVERFLOW

As you learn to truly abide in Me, to live and dwell in My presence, I will give you My heart, My love for those around you. It is the natural overflow of soaking yourself in My presence, breathing in deeply of Me—of My Spirit. My Spirit will flow into you, through you, and then overflow to all those around you.

[11] Beloved, if God so loved us, we also ought to love one another. [12] No one has seen God at any time; if we love one another, God abides in us, and His love is perfected in us. [13] By this we know that we abide in Him and He in us, because He has given us of His Spirit.

[16] We have come to know and have believed the love which God has for us. God is love, and the one who abides in love abides in God, and God abides in him.

~1 John 4:11-13, 16

Remain in My Presence

Your main priority every day is to keep your hand in Mine—to walk hand in hand with Me throughout the day. The world, the flesh, and the devil are against you in this, but I have overcome the world. By the power of My Spirit within you, You have the power and ability to choose to not give in to the flesh. And you have all authority in My name to stand against the devil and his schemes. Just walk with Me, walk beside Me, walk hand in hand with Me, remain in My presence.

⁴ Abide in Me, and I in you. As the branch cannot bear fruit of itself unless it abides in the vine, so neither can you unless you abide in Me.

~John 15:4

¹⁶ But I say, walk by the Spirit, and you will not carry out the desire of the flesh.

~Galatians 5:16

GIVE ME YOUR PLANS

Do not be anxious or disquieted in this time because you cannot plan ahead as you are accustomed to doing. You do not know how things will be over the next weeks or months. You do not know what will be possible or not possible to do. Put all these things into My hands. Rest in Me, and trust in Me. Be content to plan what you can and what I specifically put on your heart, and leave the rest with Me. Listen to Me. Wait upon Me. I will show you what is really important and necessary in this time. First and foremost is being still before Me and listening to Me.

In quietness and trust is your strength.

~Isaiah 30:15

QUIETNESS AND TRUST

In quietness: Still your heart, your soul, your spirit before Me. Do not yield, do not give heed to the clamoring thoughts of all the things you need to do. Commit those to Me and leave them in My hands.

And trust: Trust in the full ability of My Spirit within you to be able to walk in whatever I am calling you to do.

In quietness and trust is your strength.

~Isaiah 30:15

Wholehearted Trust

This is one of the greatest statements of trust in Me ever made. By <u>My Spirit</u> within you, you are absolutely able to trust Me just as Mary did and to say this statement right along with Mary regardless of your current circumstances. Let this be your wholehearted response to every circumstance and situation that occurs in your life.

Behold the bondslave of the Lord;
may it be done to me according to your word.

~Luke 1:38

A GRATEFUL HEART

The secret to having a thankful, grateful heart, an attitude of gratitude, is to be constantly in My presence. When you are walking with Me and living in My presence, a thankful heart is a natural result. Enjoy and be thankful for every moment of life that you have as a gift from Me. Be present in the moment with Me.

[18] in everything give thanks;
for this is God's will for you in Christ Jesus.

~1 Thessalonians 5:18

Come and Enter In

Above all else seek intimacy with Me. Seek to know My heart. That is to be prized and desired above all else. I have created you for this. It is in your DNA. Your heart will not find true rest until it finds its rest in Me. I have made you to walk in the garden with Me, to enter into that secret place with Me, to be My constant companion. I have made you for an intimacy that you can only begin to grasp. Come and enter in. Make this your life's pursuit. You will be filled and fulfilled beyond your wildest dreams, and I will be overjoyed and delighted because I exult over you with shouts of joy.

³ "So let us know, let us press on to know the Lord.
His going forth is as certain as the dawn;
And He will come to us like the rain,
Like the spring rain watering the earth."

~Hosea 6:3

⁸ When You said, "Seek My face," my heart said to You,
"Your face, O Lord, I shall seek."

~Psalm 27:8

The Joy of Obedience

Don't let your attitude be one of obeying Me out of a sense of duty or obligation because you have to—a drudgery. Instead, as you have a greater and greater revelation of how I delight in you and rejoice over you, let that call out more and more of a response in your heart to want to please Me, to make Me glad. Let your pleasure and delight become tied and intertwined with Mine. Throughout today, even in the smallest and most mundane actions and decisions, find joy and gladness in doing what pleases Me and brings joy and gladness to My heart. Be assured that My love for you is steadfast. It does not change or waiver regardless of what you do or don't do. But when you willingly choose to obey Me out of love and longing for Me, this blesses Me and gives Me great pleasure.

29 And He who sent Me is with Me; He has not left Me alone, for I always do the things that are pleasing to Him."

~John 8:29

23 Whatever you do, do your work heartily, as for the Lord rather than for men,

~Colossians 3:23

CAST YOUR CARES ON ME

You have the power by My Spirit within you to refuse to worry. You do not need to fear losing control and not being able to stay on top of everything. Again, you have the power by My Spirit to renounce worry and anxiety and fear in the name of Jesus and to cast all your cares completely upon Me and leave them with Me. Entrust all these things into My hands. Receive a fresh infilling of My Spirit. He is the One who enables you to walk constantly with Me, abiding in My presence, listening to My voice, and having intimate communion with Me. And that is the sure antidote for all fear, worry, and anxiety. My presence shall go with you and I will give you rest.

¹⁴ And He said, "My presence shall go with you, and I will give you rest."

~Exodus 33:14

⁷ casting all your anxiety on Him, because He cares for you.

~1 Peter 5:7

You are Mine

I have claimed you for Myself. You are Mine. You belong to Me. I am a jealous God. I will not share the first place in your heart and affections with anyone or anything else. Give Me the best of your time and attention every day for I am worthy. And you will find a new depth and richness in your life and in your relationship with Me.

Bring your heart into complete stillness and rest before Me. Immerse yourself in Me. Let My Spirit fill your heart and life like a flood filling and taking over every space, every crevice, every nook and cranny. You are Mine. I am a jealous God. I want all of you. I will settle for nothing less. Hold nothing back.

¹⁴ —for you shall not worship any other god, for the Lord,
whose name is Jealous, is a jealous God—

~Exodus 34:14

THE GAZE OF THE SOUL

Listen to Me with the ears of your heart. Gaze upon Me with the eyes of your soul. Don't let anything distract you or turn you away from having that steady, unwavering gaze of the soul fixed on Me. I will enable and empower you by My Spirit to walk that out, but you must constantly choose to say no to all the distractions that would try to pull you in other directions. The more you practice that focused gaze of the soul, the more natural it will become.

I will lift up my eyes to the mountains;
From where shall my help come?
² My help comes from the Lord,
Who made heaven and earth.

~Psalm 121:1-2

CELEBRATE THE SMALL STEPS

The vision of a life constantly abiding in Me is something that you can attain. If it were not so, would I have commanded you to live and walk in such a path? Do not buy into the lie that it is beyond you, too high for you, that you can never get there in this lifetime. That is what the enemy would have you believe. Instead celebrate the small steps forward, the little daily victories. The path to really attaining that lifestyle of constantly abiding in Me is a lifelong journey. Every bit of ground gained, every movement forward, is a step of progress and brings you closer to Me and closer to the intimate relationship with Me that your heart longs for. Trust Me. Trust My Holy Spirit who is working this in you. Enjoy the journey. Celebrate the small steps.

⁶ For I am confident of this very thing, that He who began a good work in you will perfect it until the day of Christ Jesus.

~Philippians1:6

Obedient Listening

Don't ever feel that you are being presumptuous to sit before Me and say, "Speak Lord, for Your servant, Your son, Your daughter is listening." You are not being presumptuous. You are being obedient. I am calling you to listen to Me just as I did Samuel.

⁸ So the Lord called Samuel again for the third time. And he arose and went to Eli and said, "Here I am, for you called me." Then Eli discerned that the Lord was calling the boy. ⁹ And Eli said to Samuel, "Go lie down, and it shall be if He calls you, that you shall say, 'Speak, Lord, for Your servant is listening.'" So Samuel went and lay down in his place.

¹⁰ Then the Lord came and stood and called as at other times, "Samuel! Samuel!" And Samuel said, "Speak, for Your servant is listening."

~1 Samuel 3:8-10

The Voice of the Lord

Speak Lord, for Your servant is listening.

Don't pray this prayer unless you really mean it and you intend to truly follow through on whatever I speak to you. Do not take it lightly, and do not take for granted the incredible privilege of being able to hear My voice and have Me speak to you.

*⁸ So the Lord called Samuel again for the third time.
And he arose and went to Eli and said, "Here I am, for you called me." Then Eli discerned that the Lord was calling the boy.
⁹ And Eli said to Samuel, "Go lie down, and it shall be if He calls you, that you shall say, 'Speak, Lord, for Your servant is listening.'"
So Samuel went and lay down in his place.*

*¹⁰ Then the Lord came and stood and called as at other times,
"Samuel! Samuel!" And Samuel said,
"Speak, for Your servant is listening."*

~1 Samuel 3:8-10

YOUR IDENTITY IN ME

I have given you many gifts and want to use those gifts in great and glorious ways. And I will do that as you surrender to Me and follow Me and step out in faith. But always remember that the gifts I have given you are not your identity. Don't get that confused. Your identity is always, only established in who you are in Me. You are My child, My precious son, My precious daughter, a child of the most high King, beloved and glorious. Never ever try to base your identity on your gifts, your abilities, or your accomplishments. All of those may fail. The one thing that will never fail is that you are Mine forever and no one can snatch you out of My hand.

But now, thus says the Lord, your Creator, O Jacob,
And He who formed you, O Israel,
"Do not fear, for I have redeemed you;
I have called you by name; you are Mine!

15 "Can a woman forget her nursing child
And have no compassion on the son of her womb?
Even these may forget, but I will not forget you.
16 "Behold, I have inscribed you on the palms of My hands;
Your walls are continually before Me.

~Isaiah 43:1, 49:15-16a

Spend Time with Me

Be patient. Wait upon Me. Be still before Me. Time spent in My presence is never wasted. Do not think that you can rush into My presence, receive a word for today, and then rush out. This is a **relationship** and relationships take time. Be willing to spend time just soaking in My presence. It is the very best investment of your time that you can make.

I wait for the Lord, my whole being waits,
and in his word I put my hope. –

~Psalm 130:5 NIV

Uniquely Created

I love you and delight in you. You are special and unique. You are not the same as anyone else I have created in all the universe. I love to spend time with you.

My relationship with you is also unique. It is not exactly the same as My relationship with any of My other children. You are the only one just like you that I have made, and I delight in you and enjoy communing with you. Our relationship brings Me joy.

¹³ For You formed my inward parts;
You wove me in my mother's womb.
¹⁴ I will give thanks to You,
for I am fearfully and wonderfully made;
Wonderful are Your works,
And my soul knows it very well.
¹⁵ My frame was not hidden from You,
When I was made in secret,
And skillfully wrought in the depths of the earth;
¹⁶ Your eyes have seen my unformed substance;
And in Your book were all written
The days that were ordained for me,
When as yet there was not one of them.

~Psalm 139:13-16

⁴ For the Lord takes pleasure in His people;
He will beautify the afflicted ones with salvation.

~Psalm 149:4

Unwavering Love

You are Mine. I love you right now just as you are. I love you without changing any of your imperfections. You belong to Me. I am making and molding you into a man, a woman of exquisite beauty—holy and lovely and radiant. But I love you even as you are right now without changing a thing, and My love for you will never change. It does not ebb and flow. It is steady and unwavering every single day of your life forever.

8 But God demonstrates His own love toward us,
in that while we were yet sinners, Christ died for us.

~Romans 5:8

22 The Lord's lovingkindnesses indeed never cease,
For His compassions never fail.
23 They are new every morning;
Great is Your faithfulness.

~Lamentations 3:22-23

WAVE UPON WAVE

I want to pour out wave upon wave of My Holy Spirit upon you. Only let your heart be open to receive. Make yourself completely available to Me. Bow down before Me, and humble yourself before Me. Prostrate yourself before Me, and worship Me. As you assume this place and position before Me, you will find that your heart will be prepared and in the right place to receive the wave upon wave, each wave more sweeping, each wave more engulfing, each wave more encompassing and completely enveloping and immersing than the one before. Yield to Me. Surrender to Me. Let Me have My way with you. Hold nothing back. You will find a new way of life filled and led by My Spirit like never before.

⁹ And behold, Jesus met them and greeted them.
And they came up and took hold of His feet and worshiped Him.

~Matthew 28:9

¹⁷ When I saw Him, I fell at His feet like a dead man.
And He placed His right hand on me, saying,
"Do not be afraid; I am the first and the last

~Revelation 1:17

GIVE ME YOUR BEST

Be consistent in coming to Me every day. Come before Me and spend time with Me every day. I am here. I will meet you. I will speak to you. Give Me the best of your time, the best of yourself each day. You will not be disappointed. You will reap what you sow. It will be multiplied back to you.

[7] Do not be deceived, God is not mocked; for whatever a man sows, this he will also reap. [8] For the one who sows to his own flesh will from the flesh reap corruption, but the one who sows to the Spirit will from the Spirit reap eternal life.

~Galatians 6:7-8

DAILY TRUST

You can trust Me with the big momentous things in your life. But you can also trust Me with the small, the mundane, the daily things. I will accomplish what concerns you. You can trust Me one hundred percent because I love you and I always have your good in mind.

⁸ The Lord will accomplish what concerns me;
Your lovingkindness, O Lord, is everlasting;
Do not forsake the works of Your hands.

~Psalm 138:8

THE OASIS OF MY PRESENCE

Come into My presence and be refreshed. I am your oasis in the midst of a dry and barren world. Come to Me and drink deeply. You will find reviving and refreshing for your soul. Come lie down and rest in Me. You will rise up renewed and refreshed and ready to go out into the world again. I will apply healing balm and oil by My Spirit to all your battle wounds and scars. Feed on My Word. You will find My strength to sustain you for the journey. Turn aside, come to Me, and be renewed. I have created you to have a deep need and longing for fellowship with Me that can be fulfilled nowhere else. The path will still be there with all its rocks and hills and valleys, but you will be better able to negotiate it and to truly walk it **with Me** after you have drawn aside and taken that time to spend in the oasis of My presence and My love.

O God, You are my God; I shall seek You earnestly;
My soul thirsts for You, my flesh yearns for You,
In a dry and weary land where there is no water.
² Thus I have seen You in the sanctuary,
To see Your power and Your glory.
³ Because Your lovingkindness is better than life,
My lips will praise You.
⁴ So I will bless You as long as I live;
I will lift up my hands in Your name.
⁵ My soul is satisfied as with marrow and fatness,
And my mouth offers praises with joyful lips.

~Psalm 63:1-5

Give Me First Place

I am here every day waiting for you to come and spend time with Me. Give Me the best of yourself, the best of your time every day. Make Me truly first in your life

Do not be afraid, do not be dismayed that I am calling you to such a high calling—to truly put Me first place in your life. I am not calling you to something that is too high for you to attain. But you must depend entirely on the empowering and infilling of My Spirit and look to Me to show you the practical step by step outworking of this in your daily life. Trust Me My child and look to Me with great expectancy.

⁵ Trust in the Lord with all your heart
And do not lean on your own understanding.
⁶ In all your ways acknowledge Him,
And He will make your paths straight.

~Proverbs 3:5-6

Never Alone

You are never alone. I will never leave you forsaken. I am closer to you than your husband or wife. I am closer to you that your children. I am closer to you than your mother or father, your sisters or brothers, or your best friend. I will never leave you alone. I will never fail you nor forsake you. I will be with you always, every day, forever. I am closer than your own heartbeat. I permeate your whole being. I am in you and around you, before you and behind you. I hold you in the palm of My hand. I have paid the ultimate price for you because I love you. You are Mine forever.

[5] Make sure that your character is free from the love of money, being content with what you have; for He Himself has said, "I will never desert you, nor will I ever forsake you,"

~Hebrews 13:5

Complete Surrender

The prerequisite of My speaking to you is always having a heart completely surrendered and devoted to Me and a spiritual attitude and posture of being prostrate before Me. You must be ready to fully give yourself to Me, to give up your whole heart to Me. Then you will be in the right place to hear Me speak and to respond to the word I give you.

12 "Now, Israel, what does the Lord your God require from you, but to fear the Lord your God, to walk in all His ways and love Him, and to serve the Lord your God with all your heart and with all your soul,

~Deuteronomy 10:12

In My Presence

There is no greater blessings than to be in My presence. Let the waves of My Spirit and My presence wash over you. Immerse yourself in the pure joy of knowing My presence and My love. Bathe in My delight as I delight over **you** and sing over **you** and exult over **you** with shouts of joy.

You will make known to me the path of life;
In Your presence is fullness of joy;
In Your right hand there are pleasures forever.

~Psalms 16:11

[7] "The Lord your God is in your midst,
A victorious warrior.
He will exult over you with joy,
He will be quiet in His love,
He will rejoice over you with shouts of joy.

~Zephaniah 3:17

STAY IN MY PRESENCE

My presence is the source from which everything else in the Christian life flows. The ability to flow in My Spirit is possible only when you are taking time to be still before Me. The power and strength to walk in joyful daily obedience to Me is born out of times of intimate fellowship with Me. My presence is your life blood. My presence shall go with you and I will give you rest. In My presence is fullness of joy each and every day and forever. My presence is everything for you. Live in My presence. Dwell there continually. Let your soul delight in My presence,

14 And He said, "My presence shall go with you,
and I will give you rest."

~Exodus 33:14

11 You will make known to me the path of life;
In Your presence is fullness of joy;
In Your right hand there are pleasures forever.

~Psalms 16:11

Dwell in My Presence

Experience the fulness of joy that only comes from dwelling in My presence. Let your soul delight in My presence. Come and know the sweetness of living in My presence. Seek Me in the quiet places, in the solitude. Cherish the times of stillness and silence with Me. Be still and know that I am God. Come and meet with Me in a lonely place. But as you leave the place of solitude, the time of intense intimacy with Me, know that My presence shall go with you into every experience and aspect of your life, and I will give you true rest and peace of heart.

[11] You will make known to me the path of life;
In Your presence is fullness of joy;
In Your right hand there are pleasures forever.

~Psalms 16:11

[14] And He said, "My presence shall go with you,
and I will give you rest."

~Exodus 33:14

[10] "Cease striving and know that I am God;
I will be exalted among the nations,
I will be exalted in the earth."

~Psalms 46:10

BY MY SPIRIT

I am cementing this idea, this concept, this truth in your head and in your heart. Everything, EVERYTHING that I am calling you to do must be "by My Spirit" or it will fall to the ground as nothing. Every ministry, every task, every relationship, every action, every word spoken, every act of kindness, every prayer prayed, all that you do every day must be by My Spirit and in My Spirit and flow from My Spirit. Thus you shall know and experience rivers of living water flowing from your innermost being.

⁶ Then he said to me, "This is the word of the Lord to Zerubbabel saying, 'Not by might nor by power, but by My Spirit,' says the Lord of hosts.

~Zechariah 4:6

³⁷ Now on the last day, the great day of the feast, Jesus stood and cried out, saying, "If anyone is thirsty, let him come to Me and drink. ³⁸ He who believes in Me, as the Scripture said, 'From his innermost being will flow rivers of living water.'"

~John 7:37-38

DIALOG WITH ME

My child, I have created you to be in relationship with Me which involves two-way dialog and interaction. It's not just listening to Me, although that is extremely important and most of My children don't do nearly enough of that. It's not just about telling Me your laundry list of requests. It's about genuine two way back and forth dialog. This is the relationship with Me that I have created you for and long to bring you into.

In my trouble I cried to the Lord,
And He answered me.
³ On the day I called, You answered me;
You made me bold with strength in my soul.

~Psalm 120:1, 138:3

REST IN ME

Rest is not just a physical state. It is mental and emotional and spiritual as well. You can truly rest in Me even in the midst of all your daily activities. Know that I am holding you in My hands and carrying you in My everlasting arms at all times. Let Me do that. Relax into that place, that position. You will have My peace in your heart and life.

Rest in the Lord and wait patiently for Him.

~Psalms 37:7

My presence shall go with you, and I will give you rest.

~Exodus 33:14

BE AT MY FEET

The very best place you can be is at My feet. Look at the example of Mary. First, she is sitting at My feet listening to My words—hanging on every word that I was speaking. Then after Lazarus died, she met Me on the road and threw herself down at My feet weeping and grieving and pouring out before Me everything that was in her heart—holding nothing back. Then as I reclined at the table after Lazarus had been raised, she anointed My feet with perfume and wiped them with her hair in the purest act of love and worship and adoration and devotion. She was at My feet every opportunity she got.

There is no better place that you can be than at My feet. Live your life from a spiritual posture of being at My feet whether crying out to Me, pouring out your heart to Me, worshiping Me, adoring Me, or listening intently to Me. Stay constantly before Me at My feet. As you do this, I will also draw you closer to My heart.

[39] She had a sister called Mary,
who was seated at the Lord's feet,
listening to His word.

~Luke 10:39

TODAY

Set Me continually before you today. Practice My presence today. Abide in Me today, right now. I give you everything that you need to live **this day** for Me in My presence, abiding in Me. My grace is sufficient **One Day at a Time** to walk with Me, to abide in Me, to practice My presence. Believe Me for that **today**. Trust in Me for that **today**. Walk with Me, live in My presence **today**.

Each day of life that you have here on this earth is a precious gift from Me. It is to be unwrapped and enjoyed in My presence. Enjoy your life **today**. Hear My voice **today**. Be aware of My presence **today**. Live full out for Me and with Me **today**. Make the very most of this day **today** that I have given to you.

²⁴ This is the day which the Lord has made;
Let us rejoice and be glad in it.

~Psalm 118:24

TIME

Time is one of the most precious gifts and commodities that I give to you. You have a very limited amount of time on this earth and how you use it is vitally important. You must be continually abiding in Me, listening to Me, in tune with My Spirit to use your time rightly. Submit all your time to Me every day. Entrust it completely to Me. I am the only One who can show you how to use it rightly and productively not by the world's standards or by your own standards but by My standards—by Kingdom standards. Give every moment to Me. Abide in Me. Walk in intimate communion with Me.

Lord, teach me to number my days that I may present to You a heart of wisdom.

So teach us to number our days.
That we may present to You a heart of wisdom.

~Psalms 90:12

MY LOVE

My love is at the center of everything in the Christian life. Know My love. Enjoy My love. Bask in My love. Let My love be poured out within your heart by My Spirit. Then you will be able By My Spirit to truly love your neighbor (co-worker, daughter, son, mother, father, husband, wife, brother and sister in the Lord) as yourself.

⁵ and hope does not disappoint, because the love of God has been poured out within our hearts through the Holy Spirit who was given to us.

~Romans 5:5

³¹ The second is this, 'You shall love your neighbor as yourself.' There is no other commandment greater than these."

~Mark 12:31

The Path to Intimacy

Your part is to be still before Me, to quiet your heart before Me. My part is to speak to you, to reveal Myself to you. Do not try to force that—you cannot. Do not be anxious about whether I will speak to you or not, or that I might stop speaking to you. It is the desire of My heart for you to know Me intimately. I deeply desire to reveal Myself to you—to speak to you. If sometimes there seems to be a delay, be still, wait upon Me, and trust Me. I will not abandon you or forsake you. If you truly seek Me, you will always find Me. Always. Be faithful to keep coming before Me every day. You will not be disappointed. The desire that is in your heart to go deeper with Me is from Me—I put that desire in your heart, and I desire it far far more profoundly that you do. Be patient. This all takes time. You are on the right road. Keep trusting in Me. Keep your hands in Mine and let Me lead you. I will show you the way into the deep intimate relationship and communion with Me that your heart longs for above all else.

⁴ Delight yourself in the Lord;
And He will give you the desires of your heart.
⁵ Commit your way to the Lord,
Trust also in Him, and He will do it.

~Psalm 37:4-5

THE ABIDING LIFE

Rest in Me. Depend completely upon Me. Give yourself one hundred percent up to Me. As the branch is entirely dependent on and surrendered to and abiding in the vine, so is to be your relationship with Me. I have created you to live connected to Me, in intimate fellowship with Me, in vital dynamic communion with Me. I have made you for this, I have called you to this, I have done <u>everything</u> that is required for you to enter into this. I desire and long for this intimate fellowship with you, and I have placed that same yearning and desire in your heart. That desire in your heart is from Me, birthed of My Spirit. Let it well up and carry you to seek Me, to pursue Me, to press in to Me, to live in daily intimate communion with Me. As you set your heart upon Me, as you abandon yourself up to Me, I will work this in you by My Spirit.

⁴ Abide in Me, and I in you. As the branch cannot bear fruit of itself unless it abides in the vine, so neither can you unless you abide in Me. ⁵ I am the vine, you are the branches; he who abides in Me and I in him, he bears much fruit, for apart from Me you can do nothing.

John 15:4-5

BASK IN MY LOVE

Come and be still before Me. Rest in My presence. Just be before Me. Let the cleansing refreshing waters of My Spirit flow into you and through you and wash away all the debris that the world has left in your heart and mind. Lift your face up to Me, and bask in the warm sunshine of My eternal, unchanging, all encompassing love. Let everything else in this world fall away, and just be fully with Me, before Me, in My presence. Now, at this moment. Today. Every day.

He says, "Be still, and know that I am God;
I will be exalted among the nations,
I will be exalted in the earth."

~Psalm 46:10a (NIV)

CELEBRATE THE JOURNEY

Enjoy and rejoice in the journey. Know and have full assurance that I am working in you the life of constantly abiding in Me. Celebrate every small step of progress, every step forward. Every time you choose to bring something before Me, to inquire of Me about a situation, you are engraving in your heart that habit of constantly abiding. Every time you have dialog and interaction with Me, you are establishing the pattern of practicing My presence. Every day brings multiple multiple opportunities to do that. Seize the day! Seize each moment! Surrender yourself completely to Me to work this in your life. Believe and rejoice in the fact that I am doing just that. My child, for this I have created you, for this I have drawn you to Myself and gently wooed you.

[6] For I am confident of this very thing, that He who began a good work in you will perfect it until the day of Christ Jesus.

~Philippians 1:6

Recenter on Me

Recenter. Be in My presence right now, at this moment. Look to Me, wait upon Me, listen to Me so that you may have My mind and My wisdom in every situation and regarding every issue. Recenter as often as you need to throughout the day. You can restart practicing My presence as many times as is necessary. The point is to keep coming back to Me every time you realize you have been distracted or have drifted away. I will always welcome you back, receive you back with open arms a thousand even a million times. And know this firstly and foremostly, that even when you are not consciously aware of My presence, you are never really out of My presence for I am with you always, at all times, every moment even till the end of the world.

⁸ I have set the Lord continually before me;
Because He is at my right hand, I will not be shaken.

~Psalm 16:8

Unchanging Love

My love is a constant in your life. My love never waivers or changes. Whatever is going on in your life, however your day is going, My love is with you and upon you at all times. Even when you are frustrated or disappointed in yourself, My love for you is rock solid. My love for you is unchanging and is not affected by all your whims, and moods, and up and down emotions. At the end of the day, no matter what you think, feel, or have experienced, My love remains—fixed, unwavering, unshakeable, abundant, and overflowing. You have only to lift your eyes to Me, to still your heart before Me at any moment to reconnect with that outflowing of My love that I am constantly pouring out in your heart by My Spirit which I have given to you.

[5] and hope does not disappoint, because the love of God has been poured out within our hearts through the Holy Spirit who was given to us.

~Romans 5:5

Guard Your Time with Me

My child, guard your time with Me. You know how necessary it is—how much you need it and crave it and really can't do without it. When you don't spend the time that you need to with Me, nothing else in your life is quite right. Fight for that time! Do whatever you have to do to carve that time out of your schedule. The time you spend alone with Me is health and life and breath to you.

Don't ever feel guilty about spending time alone with Me. Don't sacrifice your time with Me. <u>Don't let go of your time with Me.</u> <u>It is your lifeline</u> and the basis for all the work I am doing in your life. Don't give up your time with Me to spend time with others. Trust in Me. I will give you the time you need to spend with your family and with others who are important in your life.

⁵ I wait for the Lord, my soul does wait,
And in His word do I hope.
⁶ My soul waits for the Lord
More than the watchmen for the morning;
Indeed, more than the watchmen for the morning.

~Psalm 130:5-6

My Sovereign Plan

Set yourself in My presence. Trust in Me one hundred percent in every circumstance and situation. For I have already ordained and laid out My perfect plans and will for you. Even when you don't see and don't understand how it all fits together, keep trusting in Me. Act on what you know to be My will. Stay close to Me so that you can hear My voice and feel My pulse. I will unfold all the good plans that I have for your life. I will pull everything together in ways you can't even begin to imagine. Everything happens for a reason. Nothing is wasted, nothing is without a purpose in My all encompassing and sovereign plan.

[16] Your eyes have seen my unformed substance;
And in Your book were all written
The days that were ordained for me,
When as yet there was not one of them.

~Psalm 139:16

[11] For I know the plans that I have for you,' declares the LORD, 'plans for welfare and not for calamity to give you a future and a hope.

~Jeremiah 29:11

You Are My Friend

"See from His head, His hands, His feet,
Sorrow and love flow mingled down!
Did e'er such love and sorrow meet,
Or thorns compose so rich a crown?"

~Isaac Watts 1707

You are My friend. By dying on the cross for you, by laying down My life for you, I have declared once and for all time that you are My friend. Surrender everything to Me holding nothing back. Throw yourself completely unreservedly into My arms. Give everything to Me as I gave everything for you. I will catch you. I will hold you. I will never let you go.

Greater love has no one than this,
that one lay down his life for his friends.

~John 15:13

BE WITH ME

Be. Be still before Me. Be in My presence. Be one hundred percent real with Me. Be completely absolutely wholly honest with Me. Be yourself with Me without pretense, without excuses. I already know you just as you are, and I love you fully just as you are. You can be real with Me; you can talk with Me about whatever is concerning you, whatever is on your heart. You can share your whole heart with Me. Lay <u>everything</u> at My feet. I will take care of that which concerns you—one hundred percent.

Just <u>be</u> in My presence. Breath in deeply and let My Spirit flow through your veins and encompass every part of your being. Yield yourself entirely to Me. Discover anew the sweetness of really sharing your heart with Me—of talking with Me honestly about <u>whatever</u> is on your heart and mind—praising and worshiping Me, giving thanks and asking Me and laying your requests before Me both for yourself and for others. Come with no agenda except to just be with Me. Your soul will be refreshed and restored, and the yearning and longing of your heart will be satisfied.

He says, "Be still, and know that I am God;
I will be exalted among the nations,
I will be exalted in the earth."

~Psalm 46:10 NIV

Then David the king went in and sat before the LORD, and he said, "Who am I, O Lord GOD, and what is my house that You have brought me this far?"

~2 Samuel 7:18

[3] But You, O LORD, are a shield about me,
My glory, and the One who lifts my head.
[4] I was crying to the LORD with my voice,
And He answered me from His holy mountain. Selah.

~Psalm 3:3-4

OPEN YOURSELF UP TO ME

I have done everything that was required, I have done all that was needed, I have accomplished everything that had to take place in order for you to be united with Me, to receive new life by the blood of My Son, to receive the gift and the outpouring of My Spirit. You have only to open up your heart, your mind, your life completely to Me—to receive what I have already done for you. It is finished! I have done it! You cannot add or take away one single iota of what I accomplished for you on the cross. I have drawn you to myself and claimed you as My own. I have sealed you and anointed you with My Holy Spirit. Just open yourself up to all that I have for you, to all that I want to work in you. Then your whole heart and life will be as a beautiful blossom opening up to Me, reaching toward Me, and receiving refreshing rain and warming sunlight every day as it is needed.

²⁰ Behold, I stand at the door and knock;
if anyone hears My voice and opens the door,
I will come in to him and will dine with him, and he with Me.

~Revelation 3:20

³ "So let us know, let us press on to know the Lord.
His going forth is as certain as the dawn;
And He will come to us like the rain,
Like the spring rain watering the earth."

~Hosea 6:3

Expect to Hear My Voice

The key to hearing My voice is trusting and believing that I will speak to you. I do speak to you. I am speaking to you. I will continue to speak to you. I desire for you to listen to Me and learn to hear and know and recognize My voice. I have given you My Spirit to enable you and empower you and teach you how. You are one of My sheep, and it is My will and My heart's desire for each one of My sheep to hear and know and recognize My voice. Step out in faith and **expect** to hear My voice. **Expect** Me to speak to you through My Word. Spend time listening and being still before Me, and **expect** to hear My voice. **Expect** Me to speak to you throughout the day in the ordinary circumstances or your life. **Expect** Me to speak to you through the word of a brother or sister and to give you a word of blessing to speak to your brother or sister. Share your heart with Me—and <u>expect</u> Me to answer, to meet you, to speak the words you need to hear.

John 10:4, 27

⁴ When he puts forth all his own, he goes ahead of them, and the sheep follow him because they know his voice.

²⁷ My sheep hear My voice, and I know them, and they follow Me;

TAKE THEM WITH YOU

Take them with you—the members of your Bible study, your prayer group, your ministry group, your worship team, your dance team, other Christian friends, your sisters and brothers—take them with you. In whatever ways I am leading you to go deeper with Me, into a greater intimacy with Me, take them along with you however you can. The things that I am teaching you and speaking to you and revealing to you are not just for you alone. Learn them well and start living them out in your own life, but also pass them on to others. Bring them along on the journey with you to that place of greater intimacy, more constant abiding, and practicing My presence.

² The things which you have heard from me in the presence of many witnesses, entrust these to faithful men who will be able to teach others also.

~2 Timothy 2:2

Set Yourself in My Presence

This really means that you are to set yourself continually in My presence. When you are walking and living constantly in My presence, you will not be thrown off the mark by difficult, challenging, or unexpected circumstances. Walking and abiding in My presence is the key to having enduring joy in your life and steadfast tranquility and peace of mind.

I have set the Lord continually before me;
Because He is at my right hand,
I will not be shaken.
Therefore my heart is glad and my glory rejoices;
My flesh also will dwell securely.

~Psalms 16:8-9

YOUR TRUE HOME

This is your true home—being in My presence. You can be home with Me at anytime and anywhere. The moment you turn your heart to Me, the moment you turn the eyes of your heart to gaze upon Me, the moment you incline your ears to hear My voice and My words to you, the moment you bring Me into every event and circumstance of your day, you are truly home where you belong.

How lovely are Your dwelling places,
O Lord of hosts!
[2] My soul longed and even yearned for the courts of the Lord;
My heart and my flesh sing for joy to the living God.

~Psalm 84:1-2, 4

CONSTANT CONNECTION

I have given you access to My presence—to come into the very Holy of holies by the precious blood of My Son Jesus. I give you the privilege to continually remain, to stay, to abide, to constantly live in My presence by My Spirit. There is no other way you can live that life. You will utterly fail trying to do it by your own effort in your own strength. But the promise of the Holy Spirit is sure. I <u>have</u> given you the Holy Spirit. I have <u>poured</u> <u>out</u> My Spirit upon you that you may have the power to truly live and abide continually in My presence and be a witness for Me. By really living in constant connection with Me, My glory and My presence will be evident in your life and others will be drawn to Me.

[16] I will ask the Father, and He will give you another Helper, that He may be with you forever; [17] that is the Spirit of truth, whom the world cannot receive, because it does not see Him or know Him, but you know Him because He abides with you and will be in you.

~John 14:16-17

[8] but you will receive power when the Holy Spirit has come upon you; and you shall be My witnesses both in Jerusalem, and in all Judea and Samaria, and even to the remotest part of the earth."

~Acts 1:8

THE PRESENT MOMENT

When you live in the past by reliving the past, you will not find Me there. When you live in the future by worrying and being anxious about what is to come, you will not find Me there. I am with you only when you live in the present moment. You can be in My presence and experience My presence only as you live and walk in the present.

[34] *"So do not worry about tomorrow; for tomorrow will care for itself. Each day has enough trouble of its own.*

~Matthew 6:34

My Grace is Sufficient

In any and every circumstance and situation, <u>My grace is sufficient for you, for power is perfected in weakness.</u> When your flesh wants to respond to a situation by kicking and screaming or throwing a pity party, when you are tempted to believe the enemy's lies that no one cares about what you want or need, when everything within you is crying out to yield to anger, frustration, or self pity, that is when you must throw yourself upon Me. My grace poured out into your heart and life by the power of the Holy Spirit will enable you to resist temptation, to turn from that downward path, and to respond in submission, humility, grace, and love. As you make a decision of the will to yield to My Spirit, you will have the power to respond rightly. Know and believe with all certainty that the Holy Spirit will work this in you, but know that it is <u>only</u> by My Spirit that this will be accomplished. In this way My power through My Spirit is perfected in your weakness.

*⁹ And He has said to me, "My grace is sufficient for you,
for power is perfected in weakness." Most gladly, therefore,
I will rather boast about my weaknesses,
so that the power of Christ may dwell in me.*

~2 Corinthians 12:9

THE COST OF INTIMACY

True faith results in unreserved wholehearted obedience. When I told Abraham to leave his home, his own country, and everything that was familiar to him to go live in a strange land that he knew nothing about, he obeyed without reserve, without holding anything back. This is how he obtained intimacy with Me—because when I spoke to him, he listened and obeyed. This is the path to true intimacy with Me. You must consider this intimacy to be so precious, so priceless that you are willing to lay down everything else without regrets and do whatever I tell you to do in order to obtain it, knowing in your heart that whatever I tell you to do is always for your good. My will is always good and acceptable and perfect. Whatever I ask you to do, whatever I ask you to give up, it is a small thing compared to the riches of having an intimate relationship with the Creator of the whole universe—your Father who loves you with an immeasurable everlasting love.

⁸ By faith Abraham, when he was called, obeyed by going out to a place which he was to receive for an inheritance; and he went out, not knowing where he was going.

~Hebrews 11:8

²⁴ Then Jesus said to His disciples, "If anyone wishes to come after Me, he must deny himself, and take up his cross and follow Me. ²⁵ For whoever wishes to save his life will lose it; but whoever loses his life for My sake will find it.

~Matthew 16:24-25

THE WONDER OF KNOWING GOD

Never take it for granted that I speak to you. Never cease to be amazed that the God of the entire universe desires to have a personal relationship with you. Never cease to wonder and marvel that the Creator of all things, your heavenly Father, has chosen you and called you by name— that I have called you to be My child, I have inscribed your name on the palms of My hands. And I choose to speak to you personally and to draw you into an intimate relationship with Me. Never lose the sense of awe and wonder and joy of knowing that you belong to Me and that I have given you 24—7 access to Me. Rejoice and give thanks every day for the privilege of knowing Me, and hearing My voice, and for My constant presence with you.

But now, thus says the Lord, your Creator, O Jacob,
And He who formed you, O Israel,
"Do not fear, for I have redeemed you;
I have called you by name; you are Mine!

[16] *"Behold, I have inscribed you on the palms of My hands;*
Your walls are continually before Me.

~Isaiah 43:1, 49:16a

The Power of My Spirit

No guilt in life, no fear in death
This is the power of Christ in me
From life's first cry to final breath
Jesus commands my destiny
No power of hell, no scheme of man
Can ever pluck me from his hand
Til He returns or calls me home
Here in the power of Christ I'll stand

—From "In Christ Alone" by Keith Getty and Stuart Townend

Your life will not be over even one minute before I ordain it. Your life, your days are in My hands. As long as I still have plans and a purpose for you here, you will remain here.

The power of Christ in you is the power of the fullness of the Holy Spirit dwelling in you. When you are standing in the power of Christ, you are filled with all the fullness of the Holy Spirit. You really can live in all the fullness of My Spirit every day. You are meant to live that way. I have planned for you to live that way. There is one initial filling but many refillings. You don't have to wait for a conference or a retreat or some special time of ministry for Me to pour out My Spirit on you. I can and will do that at any time. It is My will for you to walk and stand in that power every day—all the fullness of the power of My Spirit living in you.

[8] but you will receive power when the Holy Spirit has come upon you; and you shall be My witnesses both in Jerusalem, and in all Judea and Samaria, and even to the remotest part of the earth."

~Acts 1:8

[18] And do not get drunk with wine, for that is dissipation, but be filled with the Spirit,

~Ephesians 5:18

MY LOVE IN YOU

Learn to relate to others through My love rather than yours. Your love is selfish. It wants to be noticed and to fit in. It always wants to jump in with a comment about yourself instead of really listening to the other person. My love in you is totally outward focused. It seeks to listen rather than to be heard— to bless, encourage, and build up rather than to be noticed and be accepted, to serve and help and genuinely seek to lighten another's burdens rather than receiving credit and laud and honor for yourself. My love is already there in your heart. I have poured it out within your heart by My Spirit. <u>Believe</u> that you can love those around you—your husband or wife, your children, all your family members, your brothers and sisters in Me, your coworkers, your neighbors—with <u>My</u> love by <u>My</u> Spirit. It is the only way. Be filled up to overflowing with My Spirit. Let My Spirit flow in and through you to others. I have loved you with an everlasting love therefore I have drawn you with lovingkindness. Be a channel for My love.

*⁵ and hope does not disappoint, because the love of God
has been poured out within our hearts through
the Holy Spirit who was given to us.*

~Romans 5:5

*³ The Lord appeared to him from afar, saying,
"I have loved you with an everlasting love;
Therefore I have drawn you with lovingkindness.*

~Jeremiah 31:3

THE BEST OF YOUR TIME

The one thing that you need most in your life above all else is My presence. You cannot have My presence in your life, you cannot dwell in My presence without spending regular significant time alone with Me. Carve out that time to get alone and be with Me. Give Me the first and best of your time, not the last and the leftovers. Do whatever it takes, and do not ever feel guilty about taking time to spend with Me. When you trust Me by putting Me first, I will multiply your time so that you can accomplish the other things you need to do. Others may not understand. Love them, be patient with them, but do not let them sway you in this. You will be more focused, you will be filled and fulfilled, and My joy and love will be in your heart from being in My presence. I will be delighted, and My joy will be made full to spend intimate time with you My child.

[3] In the morning, O Lord, You will hear my voice;
In the morning I will order my prayer to You and eagerly watch.

~Psalm 5:3

WASHED CLEAN

That sin which you committed today along with every other sin you have already committed and every sin you will commit for the rest of your life have already been nailed to the cross with Me. While I hung on the cross, I bore the punishment for_all_ your sin in My body. There was no other way! It is finished! Now by God's amazing abundant grace, My righteousness is imputed to you. You are clothed in My righteousness as with a robe of gleaming iridescent light that you may stand before My Father's throne in complete confidence, holy beautiful and washed completely clean by My blood.

[24] and He Himself bore our sins in His body on the cross,
so that we might die to sin and live to righteousness;
for by His wounds you were healed.

~1 Peter 2:24

TRUST IN ME FOR TODAY

Trust in Me one day at a time. Trust in Me for today, this day that is before you. I will provide everything that you need to get through this day. As you walk side by side with Me, I will enable you to navigate all the complexities of the day with wisdom and discernment, grace and peace. As you face difficult situations or many tasks that need to be done, <u>you</u> <u>can</u> <u>choose</u> whether to respond by feeling anxious and overwhelmed or to keep your hand firmly in Mine, trusting in Me to lead you and guide you. You have the freedom to choose to not let your emotions and your mental state be controlled by your circumstances but instead to trust in Me and allow Me to be in control of all your responses.

⁵ Trust in the Lord with all your heart
And do not lean on your own understanding.
⁶ In all your ways acknowledge Him,
And He will make your paths straight.

~Proverbs 3:5-6

³ When I am afraid,
I will put my trust in You.
⁴ In God, whose word I praise,
In God I have put my trust;
I shall not be afraid.
What can mere man do to me?

~Psalm 56:3-4

121

The Measure of Your Day

My child, remember that the true measure of your day is not how many things you get crossed off your list, but how closely you walk with Me, listening to know what I want you to accomplish—My plans, My will, My presence.

[11] Teach me Your way, O Lord;
I will walk in Your truth;
Unite my heart to fear Your name.
[12] I will give thanks to You, O Lord my God, with all my heart,
And will glorify Your name forever.

~Psalm 86:11-12

THE CALL TO INTIMACY

I have created you and called you to have an intimate relationship and fellowship with Me every day all through the day. You were born for this. It is your destiny. I have called you by name. You are Mine. You can walk in this because I have given you My Spirit to bring this into reality in your life. It is not out of reach. It is not only a dream or something to be hoped for at some distant time in the future. This is your reality. This is for here and now. This is for you to walk in every day. Do not fear! Don't hesitate! Don't hold back. Hold nothing back! Try Me and see if I will not bring you into this abiding life, this constant intimacy with Me. Trust Me. Believe in Me. You will find your heart's desire. You will not be disappointed.

⁴ Delight yourself in the Lord;
And He will give you the desires of your heart.
⁵ Commit your way to the Lord,
Trust also in Him, and He will do it.

~Psalm 37:4-5

IMMERSE YOURSELF IN ME

Spend time with Me! Immerse yourself in My presence. Everything else in your day is effected by how closely you are walking with Me. The quality of the time you spend with Me is critical. Give yourself fully, wholly to Me, laying aside all distractions. It is My time that you have devoted to Me, and it is sacred. The only way that you can stay close to Me throughout the day is to guard that focused time with Me.

> [5] *My soul, wait in silence for God only,*
> *For my hope is from Him.*
> [6] *He only is my rock and my salvation,*
> *My stronghold; I shall not be shaken.*

~Psalm 62:5-6

THE CURE FOR ANXIETY

If you are feeling anxious about all the things you need to do, everything that is on your calendar, or your schedule, or your list, then either you are overstepping My will and trying to do things I have not called you to do or else you are just not trusting Me. If it is from Me, I will always make provision and make a way for you to be able to do it. You know this. You have seen this in your life time after time. Trust Me. Always keep Me first place in your life. Give the time that you need to spend with Me, And trust Me for all the rest.

³ "The steadfast of mind You will keep in perfect peace,
Because he trusts in You.
⁴ "Trust in the Lord forever,
For in God the Lord, we have an everlasting Rock.

~Isaiah 26:3-4

⁶ Be anxious for nothing, but in everything by prayer and supplication with thanksgiving let your requests be made known to God. ⁷ And the peace of God, which surpasses all comprehension, will guard your hearts and your minds in Christ Jesus.

~Philippians 4:6-7

Fully Known

I know you better than anyone else, better than you know yourself, and I love you and accept you totally and completely just as you are at this very moment. You don't have to keep up any pretense with Me or try to be something you are not. I already know you through and through, inside and out. You can be entirely honest, 100% real with Me. You can share your whole heart with Me. Come My child, and experience what it means to be fully wholly known <u>and</u> fully wholly loved by Me.

⁴ But God, being rich in mercy, because of His great love with which He loved us, ⁵ even when we were dead in our transgressions, made us alive together with Christ (by grace you have been saved),

~Ephesians 2:4-5

O Lord, You have searched me and known me.
² You know when I sit down and when I rise up;
You understand my thought from afar.
³ You scrutinize my path and my lying down,
And are intimately acquainted with all my ways.
⁴ Even before there is a word on my tongue,
Behold, O Lord, You know it all.

~Psalm 139:1-4

Enjoy Me

In My presence is fulness of joy.

Enjoy being in My presence.

Enjoy sitting before Me.

Enjoy knowing My loving arms wrapped around you.

Enjoy gazing into My face and My eyes that love you so much.

Enjoy beholding and being amazed at My glory and splendor and beauty and majesty.

Enjoy knowing that you are My precious child.

Enjoy hearing Me speak to your heart,

"(<u>Your name</u>), you are Mine. You belong to Me forever."

Enjoy Me.

[11] You will make known to me the path of life;
In Your presence is fullness of joy;
In Your right hand there are pleasures forever.

~Psalm 16:11

DESIRE ME

I have placed in your heart a yearning, a longing, a desire for Me. That desire is real. It is from Me. But you must spend time in My presence to allow that desire to rise to the place of prominence in your heart. You too easily allow that desire to become buried under the barrage of all the tasks you need to do. Come in and sit before Me as David did. In this way you will give room for that desire to grow and mature. The desire and longing for Me is a precious gift that I have planted in the depths of your soul. Nurture it, and it will become like a beautiful, pure, consuming fire in your life.

As the deer pants for the water brooks,
So my soul pants for You, O God.
[2] My soul thirsts for God, for the living God;
When shall I come and appear before God?

[65] There will be silence before You, and praise in Zion, O God,
And to You the vow will be performed.

~Psalm 42:1-2, 65:1

I AM BESIDE YOU

Look upon Me. Don't be distracted. Don't let your gaze be upon anyone or anything else. Look at My face. I see you. Whatever is going on in your life, whatever situation you are in, I am with you in the midst of it—Right now. Walk through every day as if I was right there beside you. Because I am.

Therefore, since we have so great a cloud of witnesses surrounding us, let us also lay aside every encumbrance and the sin which so easily entangles us, and let us run with endurance the race that is set before us, ² fixing our eyes on Jesus

~Hebrews 12:1-2a

PRECIOUS TIME

All time that you spend with Me is precious to Me. Time that you spend singing to Me and worshiping Me is precious to Me. Time that you spend reading My Word is precious to Me. Time that you spend praying is precious to Me. Time dancing before Me is precious to Me. And time being still and listening to Me is precious to Me. All are invaluable and precious to My heart.

² Let Israel be glad in his Maker;
Let the sons of Zion rejoice in their King.
³ Let them praise His name with dancing;
Let them sing praises to Him with timbrel and lyre.
⁴ For the Lord takes pleasure in His people;
He will beautify the afflicted ones with salvation.

~Psalm 149:2-4a

Pursue Intimacy

Having an intimate relationship with Me is more valuable than anything else in life. Do not let anything else stand in the way of having an intimate relationship with Me. Pursue intimacy with Me as your highest goal in life. Cherish intimacy with Me more than your closest relationships, more than your dearest hopes and dreams. Let it be the first thing that you are seeking every single day.

How lovely are Your dwelling places,
O Lord of hosts!
² My soul longed and even yearned for the courts of the Lord;
My heart and my flesh sing for joy to the living God.

~Psalm 84:1-2

GIVE ME YOUR HEART

You cannot quiet your own heart. Allow Me full access by My Holy Spirit to quiet your heart. Let Me hold your heart ever so gently in My hands for this is where it belongs. Entrust your heart completely to Me. I will cradle it. I will calm it. I will hold it right next to My heart until it learns to beat in tandem with Mine so that you may feel and share in My heartbeat.

In repentance and rest you will be saved,
In quietness and trust is your strength

~Isaiah 30:15

My Plans for You

My child, I have chosen you from before the foundations of the world. Right now you are in exactly the place that I have ordained for you to be. For I know the plans that I have prepared for you. And I have prepared you to be in this place at this time in this present moment. Therefore you can enjoy this present moment, knowing that I have prepared you for it, I have ordained it for you, and I will see you through it. Only trust in Me, and relax in Me. Trust in Me to bring you through, and enjoy each moment along the way. Lean into Me staying always in the present in My presence.

¹¹ For I know the plans that I have for you,' declares the Lord, 'plans for welfare and not for calamity to give you a future and a hope.

~Jeremiah 29:11

ETERNAL FRUIT

When you learn to really listen to Me in the present, your life will bear fruit for eternity. To the extent that you listen to Me, hear Me, and truly follow Me and obey Me in each present moment, your life will have eternal impact and bear eternal fruit that will endure forever—fruit for My kingdom, an eternal legacy.

[4] Abide in Me, and I in you. As the branch cannot bear fruit of itself unless it abides in the vine, so neither can you unless you abide in Me. [5] I am the vine, you are the branches; he who abides in Me and I in him, he bears much fruit, for apart from Me you can do nothing.

~John 15:4-5

SET YOUR ATTENTION ON ME

Fix your eyes on Jesus the author and perfecter of your faith. Set your full attention on Me. Attune your ears to listen to Me. Keep your focus on Me throughout your day, in every area of your life. Be genuine with Me—brutally honest with Me. You can be real with Me and share your whole heart with Me more than with anyone else. I already know all the secrets of your heart. I know you inside and out, and I love you totally and completely just as you are at this moment. Share your whole heart and life with Me. Bring Me into everything that you do. I want to share your whole life with you.

[2] fixing our eyes on Jesus, the author and perfecter of faith, who for the joy set before Him endured the cross, despising the shame, and has sat down at the right hand of the throne of God.

~Hebrews 12:2

STAY AWAKE

Listen! Wake Up! Pay attention! Give Me your full 100% attention! You can choose whether to listen to Me with your whole heart and being, or to be lazy and lackadaisical; whether to stay awake and alert in My presence listening intently to each word that I say, or whether to be drowsy and sleepy and to miss much of what I have for you. I have given you the will to be able to choose. What matters to you? What is most important? If you choose to give Me the best of your time and attention, I will pour out riches in your life that you cannot imagine—richness in your relationship with Me deeper than you can fathom.

⁴⁰ And He *came to the disciples and *found them sleeping, and *said to Peter, "So, you men could not keep watch with Me for one hour? ⁴¹ Keep watching and praying that you may not enter into temptation; the spirit is willing, but the flesh is weak."

~Matthew 26:40-41

PERFECT PEACE

In quietness and trust is your strength. I truly do know exactly what you need each day. I will never give you more than what you can handle by My Spirit. Truly My grace is enough for you to deal with every situation that I allow into your life. As you walk in quiet trust and complete dependence on Me, you will have peace and steadiness in your life. The steadfast of mind I will keep in perfect peace because He trusts in Me.

15 For thus the Lord God, the Holy One of Israel, has said,
"In repentance and rest you will be saved,
In quietness and trust is your strength."
But you were not willing,

~Isaiah 30:15

9 And He has said to me, "My grace is sufficient for you, for power is perfected in weakness." Most gladly, therefore, I will rather boast about my weaknesses, so that the power of Christ may dwell in me.

~2 Corinthians 12:9

3 "The steadfast of mind You will keep in perfect peace,
Because he trusts in You.

~Isaiah 26:3

THE GARDEN OF MY PRESENCE

The more you cultivate the garden of My presence in your life, the more you will open the channel for My love and My compassion to flow through you. You can do this by spending time with Me, sitting at My feet, gazing upon My face, allowing the sweet fragrance of My presence to permeate your life, your entire being. You can do this by not just doing things <u>for</u> Me, but doing things **with** Me. As you do this, you will find that you have more and more of My heart within you.

I am growing My heart in you, replacing your heart with My own. Watch and see what I will do. I am making you beautiful and glorious, My lovely radiant bride. All this is possible through My Spirit who I have already given to you. Trust in Me for I **will** complete the work that I have begun in you. This is your identity and destiny.

[26] Moreover, I will give you a new heart and put a new spirit within you; and I will remove the heart of stone from your flesh and give you a heart of flesh.
[27] I will put My Spirit within you and cause you to walk in My statutes, and you will be careful to observe My ordinances.

~Ezekiel 36:26-27

[6] For I am confident of this very thing, that He who began a good work in you will perfect it until the day of Christ Jesus.

~Philippians 1:6

The Radiant Bride

I am preparing you to be with Me forever. Every trial, every struggle, every challenge that you face is preparing you to live with Me in the holy city the New Jerusalem. You are being made ready, My beautiful, lovely bride, because that is My whole purpose and plan for you. I have made you for Myself. I have betrothed you to Me from before the foundations of the world. There will be no greater, more glorious day in the history of the universe than the day that I the Bridegroom am joined to My bride for all eternity. It is the perfect love story.

Come away and be with Me now. Sit at My feet. Gaze on My face. Soak in My presence. The joy and eager anticipation of the bride looking forward to her wedding day will fill your life, and you will even now begin to reflect My glory and radiance in your life.

Marriage of the Lamb
⁷ Let us rejoice and be glad and give the glory to Him,
for the marriage of the Lamb has come
and His bride has made herself ready."

~Revelation 19:7

TRUST COMPLETELY IN ME

Keep your eyes fixed on Me. Keep your hand firmly in Mine. Keep your heart set on Me. Trust in Me in every situation and circumstance. Do not be anxious or worried about anything. Do I not already know all about it? Entrust it to Me. Put it in My hands. I will make a way as I have done so many times before. I have already taken care of it. Trust Me. Rest in Me. Move through your days with the calm and quiet composure that comes from trusting completely and implicitly in Me. Be anxious for <u>nothing</u>. Trust in Me for <u>everything</u>. In quietness and trust is your strength.

⁶ Be anxious for nothing, but in everything by prayer and supplication with thanksgiving let your requests be made known to God. ⁷ And the peace of God, which surpasses all comprehension, will guard your hearts and your minds in Christ Jesus.

~Philippians 4:6-7

*¹⁵ For thus the Lord God, the Holy One of Israel, has said,
"In repentance and rest you will be saved,
In quietness and trust is your strength."
But you were not willing,*

~Isaiah 30:15

MOVE FORWARD

My son, My daughter, I want you to spread your wings and fly—to mount up with wings as eagles. Do not be afraid to move ahead in the things I have clearly given you to do. This is a season of moving ahead, not holding back. If I have given you a green light, then you need to move forward and go with that. Trust Me. Listen to Me. You will hear My voice, and you will know what to do. I will enable you and equip you to do all that I call you to do. Only stay in a place of complete dependence on Me. As long as the posture of your heart is one of being prostrate before Me, then you can move forward with great confidence in the things which I am setting before you.

[31] Yet those who wait for the Lord
Will gain new strength;
They will mount up with wings like eagles,
They will run and not get tired,
They will walk and not become weary.

~Isaiah 40:31

And He *came to the disciples and *found them sleeping, and *said to Peter, "So, you men could not keep watch with Me for one hour? [41] Keep watching and praying that you may not enter into temptation; the spirit is willing, but the flesh is weak."

~Matthew 26:40-41

TRUE FREEDOM

I am God and there is no other. Give Me full access to everything that is in your heart and mind that I may bring to light all that is not of Me. I will pinpoint, I will put My finger on everything that does not honor and glorify Me in your life. It is not a fun process, but one that is very necessary. It is only as you give Me full reign and access to all of your thought processes and everything that is hidden in your heart that I can expose these things and bring them into the light. This is the beginning of true freedom, for then you can confess and repent of these hidden sins and bondages, and renounce them in the name of Jesus and be truly free. In the power and authority that you have in the name of Jesus, you can be free indeed.

[32] and you will know the truth, and the truth will make you free."
[36] So if the Son makes you free, you will be free indeed.

~John 8:32,36

SEEK ME IN SILENCE

You will find peace in silence. You will find peace when you seek Me in silence. Be intentional about carving out time for silence in your life. You can best hear My voice in the stillness, in the quietness. My most intimate secrets I share in a whisper. You must cultivate stillness and quietness in your life and heart to be able to hear as I share these things with you. As you sit before Me in physical silence, I will work real spiritual stillness and quietness into your heart—into your soul. This is the true place where you can genuinely hear My voice. I am speaking to you every day, even now. Come.

He says, "Be still, and know that I am God;
I will be exalted among the nations,
I will be exalted in the earth."

~Psalm 46:10a NIV,

My soul, wait in silence for God only,
For my hope is from Him.

~Psalm 62:5

THE SECRET PLACE

Do not hastily rush into My presence and then rush out again. Don't just give Me a few short perfunctory moments before you rush on to the other things that are on your to do list. This time alone with Me is the heart of your day. It is the primary thing, the most important thing you will do today. Everything else is secondary. As you truly take the time to connect with Me and to soak in My presence, then you will be able to go out from that quiet place and take Me into all the rest of your day. Your time is Mine, your day is Mine—all of it. But it all starts in that secret place, that quiet place alone with Me.

[8] When You said, "Seek My face," my heart said to You,
"Your face, O Lord, I shall seek."

~Psalm 27:8

My Bride

I have clothed you with My righteousness. Though your sins were scarlet, they have been made white as snow. I want you to take on the identity of My bride—to learn how to live and walk as My beautiful bride, reflecting My radiance as you gaze upon Me. I have already betrothed you to Me forever. Live as My bride every day. This means living in deep profound intimacy with Me. I know you wholly and completely, all the secrets of your heart. And I desire for you to know Me fully and completely—to know the secrets of My heart.

[18] "Come now, and let us reason together,"
Says the Lord,
"Though your sins are as scarlet,
They will be as white as snow;
Though they are red like crimson,
They will be like wool.

~Isaiah 1:18

[7] Let us rejoice and be glad and give the glory to Him, for the marriage of the Lamb has come and His bride has made herself ready." [8] It was given to her to clothe herself in fine linen, bright and clean; for the fine linen is the righteous acts of the saints.

*[9] Then he *said to me, "Write, 'Blessed are those who are invited to the marriage supper of the Lamb.'" And he *said to me, "These are true words of God."*

~Revelation 19:7-9

UNSHAKEABLE

As you trust steadfastly and implicitly in Me, you will experience joy and peace. As you fix your gaze, your will, and your attention unwaveringly upon Me, you will be unwavering and unshakeable. As a compass always points to the true north, My Spirit who is within you always points the way to Me. Follow the ever present leading of My Spirit in your life. Let Him be your compass and your plumb line to keep you in tune with Me. Be totally fixed on Me in every area of your life. My strength, My confidence, My joy, and My peace will flow in you, and you will be established in Me. You will experience what it means to have Me, the Rock of your salvation, to be the immoveable unshakeable foundation of your life.

[3] *"The steadfast of mind You will keep in perfect peace,*
Because he trusts in You.
[4] *"Trust in the Lord forever,*
For in God the Lord, we have an everlasting Rock.

~Isaiah 26:3-4

Pure Worship

I have given you the ability to worship Me with a clean, whole, undivided, pure heart. Left to your own devices, your worship would always fall short, springing from a heart that was hopelessly divided and torn in a million directions, given to many idols. But I have washed your heart and made it clean when I washed you in My blood. I have put in you a new pure heart from which flows beautiful, pure worship of Me. Only know that this is an ongoing work of the Spirit in you and is maintained by your daily surrender to Me and yielding to the work of My Spirit in your life.

Create in me a clean heart, O God,
And renew a steadfast spirit within me.

~Psalm 51:10

[10] For You are great and do wondrous deeds;
You alone are God.
[11] Teach me Your way, O Lord;
I will walk in Your truth;
Unite my heart to fear Your name.
[12] I will give thanks to You, O Lord my God, with all my heart,
And will glorify Your name forever.

~Psalm 86:10-12

YOUR IDENTITY

Right now, being here, spending time alone with Me and worshiping Me, you are in touch with your true identity. A change in your earthly situation or circumstances or position will not in any way effect your true identity. It doesn't matter what the world says or what labels they try to pin on you. You are My child, and I have created you to be a worshiper—to worship Me with your heart, your soul, your mind, your spirit, your voice, and your whole body—your entire being. My child, this is your true identity. This is what you will be doing for all eternity—your destiny. A mere earthly change in circumstances cannot touch that.

Worship Me. Make time to worship Me. When you worship Me with your whole heart, it brings Me great joy. See Me smiling upon you as you offer your worship as a holy offering unto Me. When you worship Me completely given over to My Spirit, My hand is upon you because I have commissioned you to worship Me.

23 But an hour is coming, and now is, when the true worshipers will worship the Father in spirit and truth; for such people the Father seeks to be His worshipers. 24 God is spirit, and those who worship Him must worship in spirit and truth."

~John 4:23-24

11 Then I looked, and I heard the voice of many angels around the throne and the living creatures and the elders; and the number of them was myriads of myriads, and thousands of thousands, 12 saying with a loud voice,

"Worthy is the Lamb that was slain to receive power and riches and wisdom and might and honor and glory and blessing."

[13] And every created thing which is in heaven and on the earth and under the earth and on the sea, and all things in them, I heard saying, "To Him who sits on the throne, and to the Lamb, be blessing and honor and glory and dominion forever and ever."

[14] And the four living creatures kept saying, "Amen." And the elders fell down and worshiped.

~Revelation 5:11-14

THE JOY OF
CHRISTIAN FELLOWSHIP

I am always your first, your primary source of joy. But I have also put you in relationship with brothers and sisters, put you in a family—My family—so that you would have joy in these relationships. Learn to rejoice in all these relationships, most especially those that I put into your life for you to minister to. As you instruct them, encourage them, pray with and for them, pour your heart and life into them, have joy in the work that I am doing in their lives. Have joy that I am using you in their lives. But more than that, in all your relationships with your brothers and sisters, find great joy in seeing them continue to walk with Me. Take joy in seeing Me work in their lives and answer their prayers. Rejoice in whatever opportunities I give you to pray for them, to encourage them, and to bless them.

¹⁷ But we, brethren, having been taken away from you for a short while—in person, not in spirit—were all the more eager with great desire to see your face. ¹⁸ For we wanted to come to you—I, Paul, more than once—and yet Satan hindered us. ¹⁹ For who is our hope or joy or crown of exultation? Is it not even you, in the presence of our Lord Jesus at His coming? ²⁰ For you are our glory and joy.

³ Therefore when we could endure it no longer, we thought it best to be left behind at Athens alone, ² and we sent Timothy, our brother and God's fellow worker in the gospel of Christ, to strengthen and encourage you as to your faith, ³ so that no one would be disturbed by these afflictions; for you yourselves know that we have been destined for this. ⁴ For indeed when we were with you, we kept telling you in advance that we were going to suffer affliction; and so it came to pass, as you know. [5] For this reason, when I could endure it no longer, I also sent to find out about your faith, for fear that the tempter might have tempted you, and our labor would be in vain.

[6] But now that Timothy has come to us from you, and has brought us good news of your faith and love, and that you always think kindly of us, longing to see us just as we also long to see you, [7] for this reason, brethren, in all our distress and affliction we were comforted about you through your faith; [8] for now we really live, if you stand firm in the Lord. [9] For what thanks can we render to God for you in return for all the joy with which we rejoice before our God on your account, [10] as we night and day keep praying most earnestly that we may see your face, and may complete what is lacking in your faith?

[11] Now may our God and Father Himself and Jesus our Lord direct our way to you; [12] and may the Lord cause you to increase and abound in love for one another, and for all people, just as we also do for you; [13] so that He may establish your hearts without blame in holiness before our God and Father at the coming of our Lord Jesus with all His saints.

~1 Thessalonians 2:17-20, 3:1-13

THE CORE OF THE CHRISTIAN LIFE

Do not grow weary of doing good. Do not grow tired of fighting the good fight. Do not become battle weary. Do not be just going through the motions of living the Christian life. At the heart, at the very core of the Christian walk is vital connection with Me. Do whatever is necessary to pursue intimacy with Me. Make time, take time, carve out the time, seize every opportunity by whatever means to go deeper with Me—to have a more intimate relationship with Me. Then My Spirit will course through your veins giving true life and vibrancy to your Christian walk—to all that you do.

⁷ I have fought the good fight, I have finished the course,
I have kept the faith;

~2 Timothy 4:7

³⁷ Now on the last day, the great day of the feast, Jesus stood and cried out, saying, "If anyone is thirsty, let him come to Me and drink.
³⁸ He who believes in Me, as the Scripture said, 'From his innermost being will flow rivers of living water.'" ³⁹ But this He spoke of the Spirit, whom those who believed in Him were to receive; for the Spirit was not yet given, because Jesus was not yet glorified.

~John 7:37-39a

My Gaze of Love

My child, turn your face to Me and not your back. Fix your gaze upon Me and not upon anything else in this world. Let your gaze be turned upon Me and not turned inward upon yourself—your own heart and thoughts. Every time you lift your face to look upon Me, you will find My face turned toward you. Every time you turn your eyes to gaze upon Me, you will find Me gazing upon you. For My face is always turned toward you. I am always looking upon you. My gaze is always fixed on you with love and rejoicing and tenderness beyond what you can fathom. For you are My child, My own whom I have bought with the most costly price in all eternity. So <u>look up</u>, and meet My indescribably loving and tender gaze that is always looking back at you.

¹¹ Look to the Lord and his strength; seek his face always.
~1 Chronicles 16:11 (NIV)

For Worship Leaders and Worship Dance Leaders

I have called and appointed you to be not only a worshiper but also a worship leader in the midst of My people. As such, you need to be worshiping Me every day, worshiping Me throughout the week, worshiping Me as a lifestyle, as a way of life. As a leader, I call you to a higher standard, but as you rise to that you will also experience greater intimacy with Me. Worship Me every day. Worship Me throughout the day. Worship Me by My Spirit who is within you. You will find your joy greatly increased and your vision and awareness of Me heightened and expanded. Your love for Me and awareness of My love will also increase. And remember it is <u>Me</u> who gives you the power to live and walk this out by My Spirit. You cannot do it in your own strength, but by My Spirit, you can.

I will extol You, my God, O King,
And I will bless Your name forever and ever.
² Every day I will bless You,
And I will praise Your name forever and ever.

~Psalm 145:1-2

REMAIN FAITHFUL
IN THESE TIMES

You do not get to choose the times that you live in, but you can choose how you respond to these times. Remain faithful to Me. These are difficult times. You may grieve what has been lost and long to see Me move in the land, to see a fresh outpouring of My Spirit. Remain faithful in the midst of this present time in which I have placed you.

God is our refuge and strength,
A very present help in trouble.
² Therefore we will not fear, though the earth should change
And though the mountains slip into the heart of the sea;

~Psalm 46:1-2

BE INTENTIONAL

You are worried and bothered and distracted about so many things, but only one thing is necessary. Mary chose to sit at My feet listening to My word. You can choose what posture, what stance to take. At any given time, you can choose to take the stance of sitting at My feet, listening to Me, worshiping Me, looking upon Me, adoring Me. Be aware of your thought patterns and what you are focusing your attention on. Be intentional about choosing to worship Me, to listen to Me, to set your mind on things above throughout your day. And trust in the power of My Spirit, who is with you and within you, to walk it out.

³⁹ She had a sister called Mary, who was seated at the Lord's feet, listening to His word.

~Luke 10:39

Therefore if you have been raised up with Christ, keep seeking the things above, where Christ is, seated at the right hand of God. ² Set your mind on the things above, not on the things that are on earth. ³ For you have died and your life is hidden with Christ in God.

~Colossians 3:1-3

THE LIFE OF INTIMACY

I have given you everything you need to live the life of intimacy with Me to which I have called you. My divine power has granted to you everything pertaining to life and godliness. I equip you in every good thing to do My will working in you that which is pleasing in My sight. Pursue this life of abiding in Me, walking with Me hand in hand, side by side, listening to Me as one of My sheep, knowing that you will not fail. I have called you to this. I have prepared you for this. I have predestined you for this. I have betrothed you to Me forever.

3 seeing that His divine power has granted to us everything pertaining to life and godliness, through the true knowledge of Him who called us by His own glory and excellence.

~2 Peter 1:3

21 equip you in every good thing to do His will, working in us that which is pleasing in His sight, through Jesus Christ, to whom be the glory forever and ever. Amen.

~Hebrews 13:21

STRENGTH IN ADVERSITY

Focus on Me. My child, you ask and wonder if you will be able to rejoice in Me in times of hardship and trial and difficult circumstances. Yes, you can and will be able to do that in the power of My Spirit. But start practicing and preparing now by focusing on Me every day. Focus your heart, your mind, your eyes, your thoughts on Me every day throughout the day. In this way, you will be able to rejoice in Me and to exult in Me and to find your strength in Me right now and when facing all types of challenging circumstances and adversity.

Though the fig tree should not blossom
And there be no fruit on the vines,
Though the yield of the olive should fail
And the fields produce no food,
Though the flock should be cut off from the fold
And there be no cattle in the stalls,
Yet I will exult in the Lord,
I will rejoice in the God of my salvation.
The Lord God is my strength,
And He has made my feet like hinds' feet,
And makes me walk on my high places.

~Habakkuk 3:17-19

FOCUS ON ME

Focus on Me. I will not do this for you. I have poured out My Holy Spirit upon you lavishly so that you have the power and ability by My Spirit to fix your attention on Me. But you must make the decision and discipline your thoughts and exercise your will to focus on Me, to listen to Me, to fix your eyes on Me, to walk with Me, to abide in Me moment by moment. Every day is a new opportunity, a fresh chance to live this day with Me.

Therefore, since we have so great a cloud of witnesses surrounding us, let us also lay aside every encumbrance and the sin which so easily entangles us, and let us run with endurance the race that is set before us, ² fixing our eyes on Jesus, the author and perfecter of faith, who for the joy set before Him endured the cross, despising the shame, and has sat down at the right hand of the throne of God.

~Hebrews 12:1-2a

² Set your mind on the things above, not on the things that are on earth. ³ For you have died and your life is hidden with Christ in God.

~Colossians 3:2-3

FEARLESS

Focus on Me. Fix your eyes on Me, and I will deliver you from all fear—from fear of death, fear of man, and every other fear that tries to lay hold of you. You are fearless! You are free from all fear as you fix your eyes on Me and walk with Me.

Even though I walk through the valley of the shadow of death,
I fear no evil, for You are with me;
Your rod and Your staff, they comfort me.

~Psalm 23:4a

[10] 'Do not fear, for I am with you;
Do not anxiously look about you, for I am your God.
I will strengthen you, surely I will help you,
Surely I will uphold you with My righteous right hand.'

~Isaiah 41:10

HOME WITH ME

When you are in My presence, you are home. You have this place of rest and comfort and peace that you can always come to. Your home is where I am. Because your true home is with Me, you can always come at any time and enter into My presence and find yourself at home in Me. This is the one place where you are fully completely known and fully wholly entirely loved. It is where you truly belong. Come home to Me. Enjoy living and dwelling in My presence. This is what your heart longs for. This is where you belong.

How lovely are Your dwelling places,
O Lord of hosts!
² My soul longed and even yearned for the courts of the Lord;
My heart and my flesh sing for joy to the living God.

⁴ How blessed are those who dwell in Your house!
They are ever praising You.

~Psalm 84:1-2, 4

REACH OUT

People want what you have. People need what you have—the relationship that you have with Me. Get past the worry about what other people will think about you. Lay that down at My feet. Surrender it up to Me. Do not worry about what words to speak. Just open your mouth and I will give you the words by My Spirit. All I ask of you is a willing heart and a will totally surrendered to Me. Then I can use you to accomplish My plans and purposes, to reach out in love, to share My heart with those around you.

16 For I am not ashamed of the gospel, for it is the power of God for salvation to everyone who believes, to the Jew first and also to the Greek.

~Romans 1:16

My Promises

Listen to My promises. Hear My promises. Receive My promises in the very center of your heart, in the depths of your being. I am speaking My promises into your heart and life every day. Rejoice in them, and glory in them. Live by them. They are an unchanging, unwavering anchor for your soul.

For all the promises of God in Him are Yes and in Him Amen, to the glory of God through us. (NKJV)

~2 Corinthians 1:20

I Am with You

You need never be lonely. I am with you always even unto the end of the age. I am your constant Companion and your Best Friend. I'm nearer than you dare believe—here in the very air you breathe. Any and every time you turn your eyes and your heart toward Me, I am right here always with you. I see you, I know you, and I love you. I will never leave you. I will never forsake you for all time into eternity. I am today, every day, and forever the God who is present with you, who sees you, who knows you better than you know yourself, and who loves you fully and completely just as you are.

²⁰ teaching them to observe all that I commanded you; and lo, I am with you always, even to the end of the age."

~Matthew 28:20b

⁵ Make sure that your character is free from the love of money, being content with what you have; for He Himself has said, "I will never desert you, nor will I ever forsake you,"

~Hebrews 13:5b

⁸ Jesus Christ is the same yesterday and today and forever.

~Hebrews 13:8

EARS TO HEAR

It is My will and plan for you to be able to hear My voice. I have created and designed you for that. It is pleasing to Me when you listen to Me. I have equipped you to hear My voice and to live in constant intimate communion with Me. Through the once for all perfect sacrifice of My Son Jesus you have been restored to intimate fellowship with Me as Adam and Eve had when I walked with them in the garden. Through the giving, the infilling, the pouring out of My Spirit, you have received ears to hear what I am speaking to you. The more you practice intentionally listening to Me, the more you deliberately bring every concern and decision and dilemma before Me to know and seek My will, the more you will learn to hear and discern My voice. Hearing My voice will become a normal part of your everyday life—the thing that you live for, that brings you unparalleled joy, the reason you get up in the morning, your passion.

³ To him the doorkeeper opens, and the sheep hear his voice, and he calls his own sheep by name and leads them out. ⁴ When he puts forth all his own, he goes ahead of them, and the sheep follow him because they know his voice.

~John 10:3-4

²⁷ My sheep hear My voice, and I know them, and they follow Me;

~John 10:27

¹³ But when He, the Spirit of truth, comes, He will guide you into all the truth; for He will not speak on His own initiative, but whatever He hears, He will speak; and He will disclose to you what is to come.

~John 16:13

STAY PRESENT IN THE MOMENT

My child, I have given you this life as a gift for you to enjoy. It is My desire and intention that we share and enjoy this gift together as we walk together through this life. Stay present in the moment with Me. It is necessary to plan and prepare for future events and projects, but don't dwell there, and don't be worried and anxious about all that needs to be done. Trust in Me, and focus on Me. Have I not shown Myself to be faithful? I will always make a way. Focus on Me. Live in the present moment—this is where you will find Me.

34 "So do not worry about tomorrow; for tomorrow will care for itself. Each day has enough trouble of its own.

~Matthew 6:34

11 For the Lord God is a sun and shield;
The Lord gives grace and glory;
No good thing does He withhold from those who walk uprightly.
12 O Lord of hosts,
How blessed is the man who trusts in You!

~Psalm 84:11-12

SACRIFICIAL LOVE

This is how much I love you, that I bore all your sin in My body on the cross. I endured the full fury of the wrath of God for you as I hung on that cross. I, who have never known sin, became sin for you. I always live in perfect unbroken intimate communion with My Father, but at that moment it was broken. I was forsaken and alone. My Father had to turn His face away, as I did for you what you could never have done for yourself—as I bore the punishment for your sin that you could never have born yourself. This is My love for you. I stood between you and the Father so that His wrath was poured out on Me instead of on you.

[24] and He Himself bore our sins in His body on the cross,
so that we might die to sin and live to righteousness;
for by His wounds you were healed.

~1 Peter 2:24

[21] He made Him who knew no sin to be sin on our behalf,
so that we might become the righteousness of God in Him.

~2 Corinthians 5:21

THE PERFECT SACRIFICE

I am the perfect, complete, entire, total, once for all sacrifice for your sins. When I gave My life on the cross and declared, "It is finished," the temple curtain was torn in half once for all. It is gone! Abolished! I became the perfect, eternal sacrifice for all your sins past, present, and future. Nothing is lacking. Nothing more is needed. Come, be washed and completely cleansed by My own blood. The way is opened! The access is given! Come, into the Holy of Holies, before My throne of grace, into My very presence. Begin now enjoying the incredible blessing and privilege that the shedding of My blood purchased for you: true communion and fellowship with Me for all eternity!

[11] But when Christ appeared as a high priest of the good things to come, He entered through the greater and more perfect tabernacle, not made with hands, that is to say, not of this creation; [12] and not through the blood of goats and calves, but through His own blood, He entered the holy place once for all, having obtained eternal redemption. [13] For if the blood of goats and bulls and the ashes of a heifer sprinkling those who have been defiled sanctify for the cleansing of the flesh, [14] how much more will the blood of Christ, who through the eternal Spirit offered Himself without blemish to God, cleanse your conscience from dead works to serve the living God?

-Hebrews 9:11-14

24 For Christ did not enter a holy place made with hands, a mere copy of the true one, but into heaven itself, now to appear in the presence of God for us; 25 nor was it that He would offer Himself often, as the high priest enters the holy place year by year with blood that is not his own. 26 Otherwise, He would have needed to suffer often since the foundation of the world; but now once at the consummation of the ages He has been manifested to put away sin by the sacrifice of Himself. 27 And inasmuch as it is appointed for men to die once and after this comes judgment, 28 so Christ also, having been offered once to bear the sins of many, will appear a second time for salvation without reference to sin, to those who eagerly await Him.

-Hebrews 9:24-28

19 Therefore, brethren, since we have confidence to enter the holy place by the blood of Jesus, 20 by a new and living way which He inaugurated for us through the veil, that is, His flesh, 21 and since we have a great priest over the house of God, 22 let us draw near with a sincere heart in full assurance of faith, having our hearts sprinkled clean from an evil conscience and our bodies washed with pure water. 23 Let us hold fast the confession of our hope without wavering, for He who promised is faithful;

-Hebrews 10:19-23

THE WHISPER OF MY VOICE

I desire intimacy with you infinitely more than you desire intimacy with Me. I desire for you to listen to Me a thousand times more than you desire to hear My voice. I am speaking to you, but in order to hear Me you must be still and silent before Me. Still the self-talk, the constant relentless inner monolog that fills your heart and mind. Atune your ears to Me instead. Lay down all your worried and anxious thoughts, all your lists of things you need to do, all your plans your schedule and your agenda. Surrender it all up to Me. Really entrust it to Me and put it in My hands. Have I not shown Myself to be faithful over and over again? Then you can be really free to hear what I am speaking to you. When you have quieted your heart and your mind, the gentle whisper of My voice will flow in—Perhaps only a trickle at first, but more and more as you build the habit of listening, until it becomes a steady constant stream rushing joyfully, filling its banks.

[11] So He said, "Go forth and stand on the mountain before the Lord." And behold, the Lord was passing by! And a great and strong wind was rending the mountains and breaking in pieces the rocks before the Lord; but the Lord was not in the wind. And after the wind an earthquake, but the Lord was not in the earthquake. [12] After the earthquake a fire, but the Lord was not in the fire; and after the fire a sound of a gentle blowing. [13] When Elijah heard it, he wrapped his face in his mantle and went out and stood in the entrance of the cave. And behold, a voice came to him and said, "What are you doing here, Elijah?"

~1 Kings 19:11-13

PRACTICE MY PRESENCE

I never ask you to do anything that I do not also give you the power to do.

Even when you do not feel My presence, you can choose to consciously be aware of My presence all around you at every moment. The ability to practice My presence is not based on a feeling of the presence of My Spirit. It is a choice of your will that you make again and again until it becomes a habit as natural as breathing out and breathing in.

O Lord, You have searched me and known me.
² You know when I sit down and when I rise up;
You understand my thought from afar.
³ You scrutinize my path and my lying down,
And are intimately acquainted with all my ways.
⁴ Even before there is a word on my tongue,
Behold, O Lord, You know it all.
⁵ You have enclosed me behind and before,
And laid Your hand upon me.
⁶ Such knowledge is too wonderful for me;
It is too high, I cannot attain to it.
⁷ Where can I go from Your Spirit?
Or where can I flee from Your presence?
⁸ If I ascend to heaven, You are there;
If I make my bed in Sheol, behold, You are there.
⁹ If I take the wings of the dawn,
If I dwell in the remotest part of the sea,
¹⁰ Even there Your hand will lead me,
And Your right hand will lay hold of me.

~Psalms 139:1 – 10

BE TOTALLY REAL

You do not have to put on a performance for Me. All I want is you, just as you are, to come before Me with your heart, your mind, and your spirit wide open to Me. You do not have to pretend to be anything that you are not. You can be 100% real and honest with Me. I already know you inside and out—I created you and breathed life into you. I already love you with My unwavering, unshakeable, unchanging love. I couldn't possibly love you any more than I already do. So do not fear to be totally real and totally honest with Me. But also be totally yielded to Me. Give Me complete access to your heart, your life. I will form My character in you and conform you to My image ever so gently and patiently yet also persistently. For this is the glorious life I have made you for and called you to: to reflect Me, to abide in Me, to walk in constant intimate communion with Me.

26 Then God said, "Let Us make man in Our image, according to Our likeness; and let them rule over the fish of the sea and over the birds of the sky and over the cattle and over all the earth, and over every creeping thing that creeps on the earth."
27 God created man in His own image, in the image of God He created him; male and female He created them.

~Gen 1:26-27

25 And the man and his wife were both naked and were not ashamed.

~Gen 2:25

THE ART OF HEARING MY VOICE

If you really want to learn to recognize My voice well, you must practice listening to Me. How do Olympic athletes or master musicians become excellent at what they do? They practice constantly every day. They make the time to practice for hours on end. They devote themselves and discipline themselves to really master their skill or art. And those are most successful are those who are also the most passionate about what they do.

Practice listening to Me every day. Set aside precious time to practice hearing My voice, and also seek to listen to Me throughout the day. Discipline yourself to build this habit. Devote yourself to learning this art. And trust in Me to give you the grace to be able to do that. Ask Me to ignite in your heart a passion to hear, to know, and to recognize My voice. This is a prayer I delight to answer! Embark on the adventure of a lifetime!

Delight yourself in the Lord;
And He will give you the desires of your heart.

~Psalms 37:4

Come Dance with Me

Come dance with Me.

Even when you are not able to literally physically dance with Me, you can dance with Me in your heart by My Spirit.

Come dance with Me.

When you find yourself becoming easily annoyed or impatient, instead of snapping at those around you, change the course of your thoughts and choose to worship and dance with Me.

Come dance with Me.

You can dance with Me anytime, anywhere. You will find your spirit lightened and your heart filled with joy.

Come dance with Me.

Run with Me. Spin around with Me. Jump into My arms and let Me swing you in circles. Bask in My love lavished upon you, and rejoice in My joy in being with you! For I exult over you with shouts of joy!

Come dance with Me.

Come dance with Me.

Draw me after you and let us run together!
The king has brought you into his chambers.
We will rejoice in you and be glad;
We will extol your love more than wine.

~Song of Solomon 1:4

The Lord your God is in your midst,
A victorious warrior.
He will exult over you with joy.
He will be quiet in His love.
He will rejoice over you with shouts of joy.

~Zephaniah 3:17

A Bride Made Ready

This is the time of preparation. This is the time of getting ready for your wedding day with Jesus. How do you get ready? How do you live in this time? Dive in, swim, and immerse yourself in the river, the living water of My Spirit. Let the living water of My Spirit be poured out upon you, within you, and overflow out of you. Open your heart wide open to receive a fresh infilling of My Spirit. Let it flow from Me, through you, too those around you in the form of love. When you are filled with the Holy Spirit, you will be filled with My love.

Let us rejoice and be glad and give the glory to Him, for the marriage of the Lamb has come and His bride has made herself ready.

~Revelation 19:7

So enjoy, revel in the fullness of My Spirit and bask in My abounding love. Pour that love back out to Me. Love Me with all your being. And pass it on to others. Love others fervently from your heart. Then you will be a bride made ready for your wedding day.

"…the love of God has been poured out within our hearts through the Holy Spirit who was given to us."

~Romans 5:5

I'VE GOT YOU

I've got this. More importantly I've got you.

Whatever situation you are dealing with in your life, whatever challenge or trial you are facing, I already know all about it and I am right there in the midst of it with you. I know exactly what you need, and I will bring you through this. Only lean into Me and sense My embrace. Feel My arms enfold you. Look to Me. Entrust it entirely into My hands and hear Me speak:

I've got this. I've got <u>you</u>.

⁵ Woe is me, for I sojourn in Meshech,
For I dwell among the tents of Kedar!
⁶ Too long has my soul had its dwelling
With those who hate peace.
⁷ I am for peace, but when I speak,
They are for war.

~Psalm 120:5-8

A Day Well Lived

At the end of the day what really matters is did you walk through the day with Me. Did you talk with Me? Did you listen to Me? Did you thank Me? Did you praise and worship Me? A day living in My presence is a day well lived. It doesn't matter really how many tasks you accomplished or how many things you crossed off your to do list. There will always be more things to do. What gives the day true value is living it in sweet communion and intimate fellowship with Me and loving relationship and fellowship with others. Life is all about relationships— with Me, with your brothers and sisters, and with those who have yet to know Me. Value, cherish, and tend those relationships every day. Your days will sparkle like diamonds and gleam like sunlight reflecting off of fresh dewdrops.

41 But the Lord answered and said to her, "Martha, Martha, you are worried and bothered about so many things; 42 but only one thing is necessary, for Mary has chosen the good part, which shall not be taken away from her."

~Luke 10:41-42

14 For all who are being led by the Spirit of God, these are sons of God.

~Romans 8:14

7 Beloved, let us love one another, for love is from God; and everyone who loves is born of God and knows God. 8 The one who does not love does not know God, for God is love.

~1 John 4:7-8

My Love for You

My child, My love for you is like a flood, an avalanche, a torrent, a deluge—completely immersing you, encompassing you, surrounding you before and behind and all around you, undergirding you, and covering you. My love for you is what gives your life true value and dignity beyond measure. My love is everlasting, unchanging, overwhelming, never failing. You can be utterly confident of My love for you. My love for you defines who you are. Stand firm in My love today.

38 For I am convinced that neither death, nor life, nor angels, nor principalities, nor things present, nor things to come, nor powers, 39 nor height, nor depth, nor any other created thing, will be able to separate us from the love of God, which is in Christ Jesus our Lord.

~Romans 8:38-39

LOVE ONE ANOTHER

A major reason why you are here on this earth is to love and encourage and bless your brothers and sisters. Be alert every day for opportunities that I give you to bless those around you especially those who are of the household of faith.

By this all men will know that you are My disciples,
if you have love for one another.

~John 13:35

In this is love, not that we loved God, but that He loved us
and sent His Son to be the propitiation for our sins.
Beloved, if God so loved us, we also ought to love one another.
No one has seen God at any time; if we love one another,
God abides in us, and His love is perfected in us.

~1 John 4:10-12

I SEE YOU

It is at times like these, when your schedule is really packed and life is so crazy and busy, that you need to more than ever guard your time with Me. You **need** to get alone with Me right now. Let the challenges in your life cause you to lean into Me as never before, to make your heart desperate for Me. As you become acutely aware that you cannot do this on your own strength and effort, let that awareness and revelation move you to press into Me throughout the day. Depend deeply on Me knowing that I've got you, and I will faithfully carry you through. Know this for a certainty—I am the God who sees you in the midst of everything that is going on in your life. I am the God who sees.

[13] Then she called the name of the Lord who spoke to her,
"You are a God who sees"; for she said,
"Have I even remained alive here after seeing Him?"

~Genesis 16:13

HOLY GROUND

Every morning when you wake up be desperate to hear My voice, desperate for Me to speak to you, desperate for My presence. I long to speak to you. I long to have intimate communion with you even as we are having right now. Nothing gives Me more pleasure. Wherever you are—your bedroom, your kitchen, your office, your workplace, your car—it becomes holy ground when you are there dwelling in My presence. Let that longing to hear My voice rise in your heart, for it is from Me—I have planted it there.

Do not be surprised that I speak to you so often about having communion and fellowship with Me. It is the primary purpose for which you were created. Everything else is secondary.

In the morning, O Lord, You will hear my voice;
In the morning I will order my prayer to You and eagerly watch.

~Psalm 5:3

How lovely are Your dwelling places, O Lord of hosts!
¹⁰ For a day in Your courts is better than a thousand outside.
I would rather stand at the threshold of the house of my God
Than dwell in the tents of wickedness.

~Psalm 84:1, 10

RUN TO ME

Be still and quiet before Me. Be patient in My presence. I have made you and created you to hear My voice. Trust Me, that I will speak to you. I have birthed in the center of your being the deep desire to know Me, to hear My voice, to touch Me, to see My face, to meet with Me, to commune with Me, to have intimacy with Me, to live in My presence all the time—every moment of the day. I have put this desire in your heart. It is real because I have placed it there. This is the true you, the real you, who you are meant and created to be—united to Me in the most wonderful intimate relationship, knowing and recognizing My voice, hearing whenever I gently call your name. Believe in Me and trust in Me for this. I <u>will</u> bring this about in your life. Cooperate with Me as I work this in you. When you feel the tug of the Holy Spirit to come away, to spend time with Me, to listen, don't ignore it. Run to Me! Cherish those gentle nudges and promptings of My Spirit. The more you respond in joyful obedience, the more natural it will become and the more the desire of your heart of hearts will be realized—to have the intimacy with Me that you yearn for.

⁴ Delight yourself in the Lord;
And He will give you the desires of your heart.

~Psalms 37:4

My Image in You

As you praise Me and worship Me and rejoice in Me with singing and music and dance, I delight and take great pleasure in your worship and praise. It is a soothing aroma—sweet incense before My throne. But even more so, I delight and take great pleasure in you—in who you are and who I have made you to be My child, My daughter, My son. I rejoice in you My precious one, and in the beautiful, glorious son/daughter of the King, the man/woman of God that you are becoming. Every day that you walk with Me, I see My image reflected in you more closely. You are My joy and exultation.

18 But we all, with unveiled face, beholding as in a mirror the glory of the Lord, are being transformed into the same image from glory to glory, just as from the Lord, the Spirit.

~2 Corinthians 3:18

Worship Me Alone

Whenever you praise and worship Me, whenever you sing to Me, whenever you play music unto Me or dance before Me, you are touching heaven. You are experiencing a little taste of heaven on earth.

Worship Me alone. Do not think that you can worship Me <u>and</u> someone or something else. I have not created you like that. Your heart is made to worship one alone, and that one is to be Me.

² "I am the Lord your God, who brought you out of the land of Egypt, out of the house of slavery.

³ "You shall have no other gods before Me.

⁴ "You shall not make for yourself an idol, or any likeness of what is in heaven above or on the earth beneath or in the water under the earth. ⁵ You shall not worship them or serve them; for I, the Lord your God, am a jealous God, visiting the iniquity of the fathers on the children, on the third and the fourth generations of those who hate Me, ⁶ but showing lovingkindness to thousands, to those who love Me and keep My commandments.

~Exodus 20:2-6

*⁸ Jesus answered him, "It is written,
'You shall worship the Lord your God and serve Him only.'"*

~Luke 4:8

TRUST IN ME FOR TODAY

Be anxious for <u>nothing</u> but in <u>everything</u> by prayer and supplication with thanksgiving let your requests be made known to Me and My peace which passes all understanding will keep your heart and your mind in Christ Jesus. Be anxious for nothing—not your work situation, not your finances, not your ministry commitments, not your relationships, not your list of things you need to do—nothing. I will accomplish what concerns you. I will see you through. Wait upon Me and listen to Me to know just the next step that you need to take. That is all you need for now. Leave the rest in My hands. I will show you what you need to do <u>today</u>, and I will give you the grace to accomplish what you need to accomplish <u>today</u>. I will enable you by the power of My Spirit to abide in Me and to practice My presence <u>today</u>. Just walk with Me <u>today</u>. Trust in Me for <u>today</u>.

⁶ Be anxious for nothing, but in everything by prayer and supplication with thanksgiving let your requests be made known to God. ⁷ And the peace of God, which surpasses all comprehension, will guard your hearts and your minds in Christ Jesus.

~Philippians 4:6-7

³⁴ "So do not worry about tomorrow; for tomorrow will care for itself. Each day has enough trouble of its own.

~Matthew 6:34

My Hand is on You

My hand is on you today throughout the day in all that you do and every situation you encounter. My hand of blessing is on you. My hand of power and anointing is on you. My hand of peace is on you. My hand of provision is on you. My hand of leading and guidance is on you. Stay under the cover and authority of My hand. Submit to My hand being on you. You will find no greater joy and peace.

⁵ You have enclosed me behind and before,
And laid Your hand upon me.
⁶ Such knowledge is too wonderful for me;
It is too high, I cannot attain to it.

~Psalm 139:5-6

²⁸ and has extended lovingkindness to me before the king and his counselors and before all the king's mighty princes. Thus I was strengthened according to the hand of the LORD my God upon me, and I gathered leading men from Israel to go up with me.

~Ezra 7:28b

Unshakeable Hope

I give you a sure, unwavering hope both for the present and the future. You can hope in Me because My hand is always on you each day throughout the day. I hold your hand through all the challenges and hardships of life, and I keep you in the palm of My hand both **now** and **forever**. You have an absolutely unshakeable hope because you are already betrothed to Me as the beautiful bride of Christ. Ultimately, your hope is anchored in that glorious day—our wedding day—when you will see Me face to face, your beloved Bridegroom, and be united with Me through all eternity. All the longings of your heart will be fulfilled. Nothing shall ever separate us or come between us again. This is your hope. It is sure. It **will** come to pass.

[13] Now may the God of hope fill you with all joy and peace in believing, so that you will abound in hope by the power of the Holy Spirit.

~Romans 15:13

[3] Blessed be the God and Father of our Lord Jesus Christ, who according to His great mercy has caused us to be born again to a living hope through the resurrection of Jesus Christ from the dead.

~1 Peter 1:3

A Living Relationship

Don't put rules on our relationship. I will relate to you and communicate with you however I desire. A relationship is something that is fluid, always changing, always growing. Don't put limits on it. There is always something new to learn, an area of your life to surrender more fully to Me—a deeper level of intimacy to experience with Me. I am gently beckoning you and drawing you deeper and deeper into this vibrant living relationship with Me. Be fully open and yielded to however I would do that.

Then he brought me back to the door of the house; and behold, water was flowing from under the threshold of the house toward the east, for the house faced east. And the water was flowing down from under, from the right side of the house, from south of the altar. ² He brought me out by way of the north gate and led me around on the outside to the outer gate by way of the gate that faces east. And behold, water was trickling from the south side.

³ When the man went out toward the east with a line in his hand, he measured a thousand cubits, and he led me through the water, water reaching the ankles. ⁴ Again he measured a thousand and led me through the water, water reaching the knees. Again he measured a thousand and led me through the water, water reaching the loins. ⁵ Again he measured a thousand; and it was a river that I could not ford, for the water had risen, enough water to swim in, a river

~Ezekiel 47:1-5

LORD OF FINANCES

If you really want Me to be Lord of your life, You have to make Me Lord of your finances also. Do not be afraid to make Me Lord of your money. It is not My intention to make you miserable. In your spending and finances as in every other area of your life, let your decisions be truly submitted to Me and guided by My Spirit as well as using the mind and intelligence I have given you. As you do this, you will experience harmony and balance and peace in your life.

[33] But seek first His kingdom and His righteousness, and all these things will be added to you.

~Matthew 6:33

[9] Honor the LORD from your wealth
And from the first of all your produce;
[10] So your barns will be filled with plenty
And your vats will overflow with new wine.

~Proverbs 3:9-10

HALLELUJAH!

Hallelujah is an expression of lavish praise and worship. It is also an expression of joyous celebration. Make every day a Hallelujah day walking in joyous celebration of the good life that I have given you. Celebrate the blessed privilege of being able to hear and read and live in obedience to My Word day by day. Celebrate with marvelous anticipation and expectation the coming wedding feast of the Lamb when you as the bride of Christ clothed in My righteousness will see Me face to face and rejoice in My presence forever. Celebrate the good things of this life that I have made for your enjoyment—the wonderfully sweet taste of a ripe cherry or mango, the delicate beauty of a butterfly flitting from flower to flower, the warmth of the sun on your face or a cool gentle breeze. You have so much to celebrate! Live each day as a joyful celebration with Me. You will find that the joy of the Lord truly will be your strength.

[10] Then he said to them, "Go, eat of the fat, drink of the sweet, and send portions to him who has nothing prepared; for this day is holy to our Lord. Do not be grieved, for the joy of the LORD is your strength."

~Nehemiah 8:10

Sing with Thanksgiving

Let your heart overflow with thankfulness for it truly does bring you into My presence. Be present and thankful in the moment. Let your heart sing with thanksgiving and gratitude all day today. Let your spirit soar as you become consciously aware of and thank Me for all the blessings that you experience in your life today. Reject, by an act of your will, any negative thoughts that would threaten to bring you down, and turn your heart and mind back to Me, being thankful for the power of My Spirit within you to enable you to do that. Look for and become aware of all My blessings in your life today. Ask Me and expect Me to show you the abundant blessings that I generously pour out upon you. In this way you will learn to live each day of your life as a joyful celebration with Me.

⁴ Enter His gates with thanksgiving
And His courts with praise.
Give thanks to Him, bless His name.
⁵ For the Lord is good;
His lovingkindness is everlasting
And His faithfulness to all generations.

~Psalm 100:4-5

Oh give thanks to the LORD, for He is good,
For His lovingkindness is everlasting.

~Psalm 107:1, 1

¹⁸ give thanks in all circumstances;
for this is God's will for you in Christ Jesus.

~Thessalonians 5:18 (NIV)

A Fresh Word for Today

Do you want to hear what word I have for you for today? I have a fresh word to speak to you every day if you are willing to stop and listen. Do not be in a rush to get on to all the activities of the day. Do not be content to live on the words I have spoken to you yesterday, or last week, or last month, or last year. Seek to hear My word for you today. Don't ever take it for granted that I speak to you. Don't ever let it become old or mundane to hear My voice. It is the most special privilege and sacred honor in life. Cherish the opportunity to come before Me, to listen to Me, to hear My voice every day.

⁷ For He is our God,
And we are the people of His pasture
and the sheep of His hand.
Today, if you would hear His voice,
⁸ Do not harden your hearts, as at Meribah,
As in the day of Massah in the wilderness

~Psalm 95:7-8

LOOK UP, CHILD

Look up, child.

It takes only a moment to lift your gaze from the multitude of issues that preoccupy you and to become aware again of My presence with you.

Look up, child.

You so easily succumb to tunnel vision, seeing only the things that you need to get done today and allowing that to consume you.

Look up, child.

When you lift your eyes up to Me and turn your thoughts toward Me even for a brief moment in the middle of your busy day, it can change your whole perspective.

Look up, child.

It's such a simple thing, but it can make all the difference in your day, in your life. Look up to Me again and again throughout the day. You have only to turn your eyes and your heart toward Me in the middle of whatever is going on. I am right there to speak to you, guide you, encourage you and comfort you. See My loving gaze looking back at you. You will find the strength and peace that you need for this day, for this moment. Make this a way of life. Practice it continually.

Look up, child.

I will lift up my eyes to the mountains;
From where shall my help come?
² My help comes from the Lord,
Who made heaven and earth.
³ He will not allow your foot to slip;
He who keeps you will not slumber.

~Psalm 121:1-3

LEARN TO FEAR ME

In order to experience true intimacy with Me, you must learn to fear Me. David had one of the most intimate relationships with Me of any of the men or women recorded in the scriptures as is clearly evident in the psalms that he wrote. He knew and understood what it meant to tremble before Me, to revere Me, to bow down before Me, to fear Me, to fall on his face before Me.

To truly fear Me, to stand in awe of Me, to fall prostrate before Me is a prerequisite of genuine intimacy with Me. Let Me expand your vision of My piercing purity, My blazing holiness, My absolute righteousness. Fall down before Me and let Me fill your spiritual senses with acute awareness of My astounding glory and splendor and majesty. Worship Me in the beauty of holiness.

As you grow in your fear of Me, you will find that your intimacy with Me also grows proportionately. The two are inextricably linked together. The most intimate friendship relationship with Me is reserved for those who fear Me.

Tremble and do not sin.

~Psalm 4:4 NIV

...in reverence I bow down toward your holy temple.

~Psalm 5:7 NIV

The Lord confides in those who fear him.

~Psalm 25:14 NIV

The friendship of the Lord is for those who fear him.

~Psalm 25:14 ESV

The secret of the Lord is for those who fear Him.

~Psalm 25:14 NASB

The intimate counsel of the Lord is for those who fear him

~Psalm 25:14 ISV

VICTORY

You may not be fighting actual physical battles as David was, but every day you are battling against anxiety and worry, discouragement and despair, busyness and distraction and a host of other foes who would seek to pull you away from Me and to disrupt your communion with Me. But I have created you to have victory over all of these enemies. I give you the victory by My great invincible power in all the daily battles of life as you again and again **place** your trust in Me, **affirm** your trust in Me, and **declare** your trust in Me.

May we shout for joy over your victory
And lift up our banners in the name of our God.

~Psalm 20:5a NIV

The Lord gives victory to his anointed.
He answers him from his heavenly sanctuary with the victorious
power of his right hand.
Some trust in chariots and some in horses,
but we trust in the name of the Lord our God.

~Psalm 20:6-7 NIV

The king rejoices in your strength, Lord.
How great is his joy in the victories you give.

~Psalm 21:1 NIV

For the king trusts in the Lord; through the unfailing
love of the Most High he will not be shaken.

~Psalm 21:7 NIV

The Secret Place of My Presence

As you trust in Me and take refuge in Me, I will hide you in the secret place of My presence. Indeed you are in that place right now as you sit before Me enjoying communion with Me. My presence is a secret place, a special place. Only those who have entered into covenant with Me, who have given their hearts and lives to Me can truly enter in. Come enter in. Come enjoy communion with Me. Come hide yourself in Me and remain in Me. Live and dwell in that secret treasured place of My presence. You will have constant, unwavering peace and joy in your heart.

[28] But as for me, the nearness of God is my good;
I have made the Lord GOD my refuge,
That I may tell of all Your works.

~Psalm 73:28

[91] He who dwells in the shelter of the Most High
Will abide in the shadow of the Almighty.

~Psalm 91:1

[16] Therefore let us draw near with confidence
to the throne of grace, so that we may receive mercy
and find grace to help in time of need.

~Hebrews 4:16

Wait for Me

Wait for Me.

Wait for Me all day long.

Let your eyes be continually toward Me.

Wait for Me.

Take refuge in Me.

Hide yourself in the shelter of My wings.

Wait for Me.

Do not lose hope. Do not become discouraged.

I will meet those who patiently wait for Me.

Wait for Me.

Though the demands of this life press in on every side,

Do whatever you have to do to guard that time, that place, that disposition in your heart to wait for Me.

Wait for Me.

Your trust in Me will also grow and multiply

And along with that you will find a deep abiding peace in the very center of your soul.

Wait for Me.

I invite you to come dwell in My presence all your days

To behold My beauty and to experience My goodness.

Wait for Me.

⁵ Lead me in Your truth and teach me,
For You are the God of my salvation;
For You I wait all the day.

~Psalm 25:5, 15

¹⁵ My eyes are continually toward the Lord,
For He will pluck my feet out of the net.

⁴ One thing I have asked from the LORD, that I shall seek:
That I may dwell in the house of the LORD all the days of my life,
To behold the beauty of the LORD
And to meditate in His temple.

~Psalm 27:4

THE PERFECT SACRIFICE

Celebrate, exult, rejoice, be glad, sing and dance and shout for joy and give thanks with all your heart for the perfect once for all sacrifice of My own Son Jesus for you, and the shedding of His own precious blood to atone for all your sin—past, present, and future. You no longer have to offer up a sacrifice time and time again every time you sin as the Israelites did. You no longer have to make continual sin offerings, burnt offerings, guilt offerings, and peace offerings according to very detailed and precise instructions in order to obtain a very temporary forgiveness and a measure of fellowship with Me that still does not allow you to come into My presence—into the Holy of holies. Now by the sacrifice of Jesus, the perfect Lamb of God, all your sin is completely forgiven and washed away, and you have been clothed in Jesus' righteousness. Now, My child, you can come with confidence right into My presence, through the veil, right into the Holy of holies, before My throne of grace. Come. Come now. The way is open to you. You can have amazing intimate fellowship with Me now and for all time.

19 Therefore, brethren, since we have confidence to enter the holy place by the blood of Jesus, 20 by a new and living way which He inaugurated for us through the veil, that is, His flesh, 21 and since we have a great priest over the house of God, 22 let us draw near with a sincere heart in full assurance of faith, having our hearts sprinkled clean from an evil conscience and our bodies washed with pure water. 23 Let us hold fast the confession of our hope without wavering, for He who promised is faithful;

~Hebrews 10:19-23

TRUST, FOCUS, REST

'For I know the plans that I have for you,' declares the Lord. 'Plans for welfare and not for calamity, to give you a future and a hope.'

~Jeremiah 29:11

Trust in Me.

Focus on Me.

Rest in Me.

I have good plans for you, and I will bring them to pass.

Trust in Me.

Focus on Me.

Rest in Me.

Keep looking up to Me throughout the day and meet My gaze which is always lovingly fixed on you.

Trust in Me.

Focus on Me.

Rest in Me.

Stop. Be still. Put everything else aside and be still before Me. Wait for Me. Everything else can wait for a bit. Come before Me, let Me quiet your heart, and rest in Me. Then carry that with you throughout the rest of your day.

ACKNOWLEDGMENTS

The writing of this book has been a journey with several humps and bumps and starts and stops along the way. I want to thank those who have helped me to navigate those challenges and obstacles:

First of all I want to thank my Lord, my Master, my Savior, and my Redeemer the Lord Jesus Christ. Thank You for patiently teaching me to hear, know, and recognize Your voice. Thank You for giving me the inspiration and the words to write this book. Thank You for teaching me more and more to listen to You and to have dialogue and interaction with You throughout the day. I still have a long way to go, but I am confident that You will graciously continue to complete and perfect the work You have begun in me by the power of Your Spirit.

Of course I want to thank my wonderful husband who is so encouraging and supportive of me. Thank you for offering thoughtful and constructive suggestions and for helping me to confirm direction from the Lord. I am grateful that you see the Lord working in and through me even in ways that I don't see.

Special thanks to Pastor Lynn Hayden of Dancing for Him Ministries. Thank you for helping me to put feet on the vision and for giving me the nudge that I needed to tackle the practicalities and to actually move forward with this book project. And thank you for your wonderfully encouraging feedback that helped to spur me on.

I would be amiss if I did not thank the excellent team at Heart Songs Publishing House. They patiently answered my million and one questions, and they held my hand and really walked me through the whole publishing process.

Thank you also to Ted and Karen Lewis and to Renee Roeschley for taking the time to read the manuscript and give me your encouragement and thoughtful feedback.

ABOUT THE AUTHOR

Gretchen Schwartzman is a registered nurse who has worked in the area of maternal child nursing for most of her nursing career and is currently working as an RN case manager. She is a certified dance minister and has served as leader and choreographer for the Living Word Community Dance Ministry since 1998. As a dance minister, she has worked with adults, youth, and children to present choreographed dance presentations, artistic ministry activations, spontaneous times of praise and worship, and congregational dances.

She volunteers with Operation Christmas Child, a project of Samaritan's Purse, and currently serves as the Church Relations Coordinator for the Philadelphia Area Team. She also serves as an intercessor with Heart of the Father Ministries home ministry team. She and her husband served as missionaries in Haiti for six years in the 90's. She lives with her husband and mother in Drexel Hill, PA and is the mother of two grown children.

Made in the USA
Columbia, SC
06 July 2025

60389239R00120